P9-CDX-467

# SGMA

# SPORT APPAREL DICTIONARY
# OF PERFORMANCE FIBERS,
# FABRICS AND FINISHES

SPORTING GOODS MANUFACTURERS ASSOCIATION
200 CASTLEWOOD DRIVE/NORTH PALM BEACH, FL 33408
(561) 842-4100 FAX: (561) 863-8984

# SGMA SPORT APPAREL DICTIONARY OF PERFORMANCE FIBERS, FABRICS AND FINISHES

Published by:

Sporting Goods Manufacturers Association

200 Castlewood Drive

North Palm Beach, FL 33408

Copyright© Sporting Goods Manufacturers Association, 1997

First Printing - 1997

Library of Congress Catalog Card Number: 97-62070

ISBN 0-9660699-0-0

Printed in the United States of America

All rights reserved. No part of this book may be reproduced or transmitted in any form or by any means, electronic or mechanical, including photocopying, recording, or by any information storage and retrieval system without written permission from both the author/publisher, except for the inclusion of brief quotations in a review.

# CREDITS AND ACKNOWLEDGMENTS

Every document as complex and far reaching as the **SGMA SPORT APPAREL DICTIONARY OF PERFORMANCE FIBERS, FABRICS AND FINISHES** is the product of the efforts and concern of many people and the guidance given by preceding authors and authoritative sources that have contributed the elements that make up the book. To them, the SGMA gives heartfelt thanks for their input, support, professionalism, interest, and encouragement. Without their efforts and previous work, this book could not have evolved into the useful document we anticipate and trust it will be. Most noteworthy of those, but by no means all, who contributed to this work are as follows:

The **SGMA Sports Apparel Product Council (SAPC)** and the **SGMA Fiber and Fabric Committee** who, with their support and approval, funded the Dictionary from the net revenues earned by members of the Sports Apparel Products Council through a grant from **THE SUPER SHOW®**, approved by the SGMA Board of Trustees.

Members of the SGMA Fiber and Fabric Committee who conceived the project and provided editorial oversight include:

Amoco Fabrics & Fibers Company
E. I. DuPont de Nemours and Company
Liberty Fabrics, Inc.
Reflective Technologies, Inc.
Sporting Goods Manufacturers Association
Summit Knitting Mills, Inc.
Trevira
W. L. Gore & Associates, Inc.

**SGMA would like to acknowledge the following technical and source contributions:**

Sportstyle Magazine
Joseph's Introductory Textile Science - Hudson, Clapp & Kness
The Encyclopedia of Textiles
Dr. Charles Tomasino - North Carolina State University, School of Textiles
Dr. Peyton B. Hudson-Textile & Apparel Consultant

**For performance illustration guidance, SGMA extends thanks to:**

Allied Signal, Inc.
E.I. DuPont de Nemours and Company
Malden Mills Industries, Inc.
Patagonia, Inc.
Schoeller Textil U.S.A., Inc.
Toray, America
Trevira
W. L. Gore & Associates, Inc.

Also, SGMA wishes to thank all trademark owners listed in the dictionary for their participation.

**Writer: David C. Kapp**
**Editor: Maria Stefan**
**Designer & Illustrator: Hal Just**

The **SPORTING GOODS MANUFACTURERS ASSOCIATION (SGMA)** is a trade association of more than 2,000 manufacturers and national brand distributors of sport apparel, athletic footwear and sporting goods equipment. It owns and operates **THE SUPER SHOW®**, the largest sports product and activewear show in the world. Net revenues earned from the show provide $5 million annually to support increased sports, recreation and fitness activities and industry growth and vitality.

# SGMA SPORT APPAREL DICTIONARY
# OF PERFORMANCE FIBERS, FABRICS & FINISHES

# SGMA SPORT APPAREL DICTIONARY OF PERFORMANCE FIBERS, FABRICS & FINISHES

## PERFORMANCE DIAGRAMS

**W**elcome to the world of performance in sport apparel. In creating this Dictionary of Performance Fibers, Fabrics and Finishes, SGMA has created a "road map" to help you better understand the many technical features that are being built into today's activewear that not only let you look good but feel good in almost any weather condition or at nearly any activity level. Also, we want you to know the many product brand names for each type of performance need you may have, who owns them, what they do, how they work and where you can get further information about them.

# A NEW DICTIONARY
# FOR A NEW ERA OF
# PERFORMANCE ACTIVEWEAR

**W**e are in the middle of a revolution in performance technology. There are a great number of products out there that are ready to satisfy nearly all your needs for apparel performance. Lightweight and strong? They are there. Comfortable and durable? Sure! Waterproof, windproof and breathable? You bet. What do you need to stay cool or to stay warm? It's all here in our Dictionary and it is all out there in the stores ready for you today.

**W**e have written this Dictionary in easily understandable terms and we have created some diagram illustrations to help you visualize how several of these technologies actually work for you.

 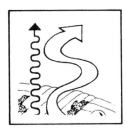 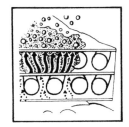

**W**e have grouped the main descriptions of the branded products under the primary purpose for which they are intended, such as insulation, moisture management, etc.

**W**e have also cross referenced many of the products with multiple features into those other categories where they also fit.

**I**n addition, we have tried to make it easy for you to find any trademark and/or trademark owner throughout the book through cross referenced listings and we have given you the full addresses, phone and fax numbers of all the listed proprietors should you wish to contact them for any reason.

**A**t the same time, we want to give you the information that will help you better understand some of the basic physical mechanisms of the body and the environment that the products here were conceived and created to address. Also, there is an excellent "Glossary of Terms" in the back of the book that may help you to understand the terminology within. We hope you find it helpful.

**P**lease understand that it is not our intention to rate or classify these products in any way concerning their performance, durability or quality. We are passing on to you the claims and descriptions of these products as supplied to us by the trademark and product owners. Our sole purpose is to provide you with the most comprehensive, easy-to-use guide and "map" through the maze of products in the marketplace. Also, we intend to periodically update this book to keep it current with the latest in performance apparel products.

**ONE LAST NOTE:**

Recently, there have been some apparel products appearing in stores that are claiming to be "performance" apparel when they do not meet any performance standard whatsoever and have no right to make such claims. Many of these products look like authentic, performance wear, but are not made of the "right stuff" to qualify for that claim.

**REMEMBER: "BUYER BEWARE"!**

Our strong recommendation is to stick with the branded performance products and apparel in the marketplace, such as the products listed in our Dictionary, or ask your retail source for guidance.

---

## NOW WE INVITE YOU TO VISIT OUR WORLD OF

---

## PERFORMANCE FIBERS, FABRICS AND FINISHES.

---

## ENJOY YOUR VISIT!

---

The concept of performance textiles and apparel is not new. In fact, historically, it would be easy to trace all sorts of "performance" apparel back to the invention of armor and when fringed "buckskins" were designed by the Indians to help shed unwanted rainwater. However, in those days, "performance" meant the difference between life and death. Today, in most cases, "performance" in apparel means ease of movement and care, comfort in all conditions and/or assistance to improve performance in aerobic and sporting activities while still looking good.

# THE COMPLEX WORLD OF COMFORT AND PERFORMANCE

We tend to forget that the concept of mass marketing "performance" fabrics and garments is a new concept. Even as late as the early 1960's, real performance activewear was only available from narrow, very highly priced retail organizations scattered around large metropolitan areas where people with wealth lived who could afford to go on Safari, to climb the Alps or to compete in the great Newport sailing regattas.

Certainly, excellent quality hunting, fishing, hiking and camping apparel and accessories have always been available, but at a cost that was usually beyond the normal "working class" pocketbook without great sacrifice. The great "sea" change came after World War II with the Baby Boomers and the global success of the "American Way" that shifted us from a "make do", post-Depression, agrarian, smokestack society into an affluent, urbanized, "tuned in", "turned on" technological society. America was "homogenized" by advertising, television. We shifted our economy from a laboring, hourly manufacturing society to a service-oriented economy and created new generations of young, affluent, credit card-bearing people who were hyped by Madison Avenue to be the "Me Generation" with "eternal youth" as a social goal and focus for the society and the leisure time to do it.

## LOOK YOUNG, STAY YOUNG, STAY FIT, GET ACTIVE AND GET OUT THERE EVERY CHANCE YOU GET.

**O**riginally, there was only a small group of international performance apparel companies who were positioned to supply the growing demand for warmer, dryer, cooler, stronger, breathable, stretchable, functional, good looking apparel. Over the past 10 years, more and more innovative performance apparel and textile sources have evolved, serving the market with a very broad variety of products for nearly every known active and sporting activity.

**I**n spite of the great diversity of the activities and sports activities these products are designed to serve, nearly all of them discussed in our Dictionary (except for "Special Products") relate to two basic needs of everyone who participates in an active lifestyle.

**I**f we take all these performance needs and boil them down, in general, one or both of the following bodily functions are being addressed:

**THE NEED TO MAINTAIN THE INTERNAL TEMPERATURE OF THE BODY WITHIN CERTAIN ACCEPTABLE LIMITS** in spite of all forms of exertion the body may experience or no matter how severe external conditions may become.

**THE NEED TO MANAGE THE MOISTURE PRODUCED BY THE BODY** through the skin to cool itself (liquid or vapor) in order to maintain a perceived comfort balance between feeling "comfortable" and dry and/or warm or cool, depending upon the external conditions and without stressing the body's fluid supply.

13

**W**e wear clothes, not fibers, fabrics or finishes. Although the focus of this book is on the special performance of the textiles that make up the clothing we wear, we need to talk a bit about the importance of the garment design as a key element in the total performance "package".

# COMFORT BY DESIGN DRESSING THE PART

**A**side from color and fashion styling decisions about clothes, selecting the right <u>type</u> of garment for your selected activity or sport is very important, both in the way the garment has been designed for that activity as well as selection of the proper fabric for the purpose. The whole equation of comfort and performance must be considered before this selection is made. There is a great difference between choosing the clothes for a tennis match versus the clothes you would need to climb Everest. However, your success or failure on the tennis court in a long, hard match in hot weather and your survival on the mountain in a blizzard may very much depend upon your garment design and fabric selection.

**U**sually, performance garments are seldom used by themselves, but rather in association with other garments that are designed for specialized uses (such as special underwear or support garments, and sports bras or compression shorts, etc.).

**In warm weather, loose, lightweight garments made with open fabric constructions and absorbent or moisture transfer materials are critical to comfort. In cold conditions, layering is the key to dryness, comfort and warmth using special absorbent or efficient wicking underwear, insulating tops and bottoms using fiberfill, double-brushed fabrics for insulation and a tightly woven shell fabric that may be coated or laminated to some sort of windproof, waterproof, but breathable material.**

**H**ats and hoods stop warm air from escaping through the head area while drawstrings and/or buttoned or "velcro" closures snug down the neck and face areas to prevent cold winds from sapping heat. Cuff areas are kept tight and drawstrings or elastic bands cinch the waist area to prevent escape of heat or the entry of cold drafts. Front placket closures become security systems by combining overlapping fabric flaps with zippers, buttons and velcro to secure the front opening of the garment and some garments even have drawstrings to "snug-up" the bottom edge of the jacket to help keep your lower regions cozy. And all of this has been done BEFORE any fabric considerations are made that address the waterproof aspects of this garment **system**.

---

**This is what we mean by "COMFORT BY DESIGN". It is the combination of garment design and performance fibers, fabrics and finishes that will provide you with the comfort, fit and performance you seek in activewear. Later in this book, we will offer you a list of all the products we have included in our Dictionary with the end uses their owners have suggested for their use. The section is called "GETTING IT ON". Don't miss it!**

---

**These are not fabrics, nor are they garments - they are:**

# COMFORT AND SURVIVAL SYSTEMS

There are a combination of a number of specialized, performance products, each intended to be combined with another or a number of other products to create a working **system** of apparel to keep you warm or cool, warm and dry or cool and dry, depending upon your needs, the climate conditions and your level of physical activity (ies).

The proper marriage of fabric(s) and garment design is the secret of real performance success in exercise or sporting activities. Excellent, high quality, high tech fabrics are wasted if they are styled into a poorly designed and poorly made garment. Likewise, a well made and well designed garment can fail without the use of proper performance fabrics.

Remember that the control of body heat and moisture are the primary keys to comfort, performance and, sometimes, survival. Garment designs for warm conditions demand ventilation, moisture management and lack of constriction at the neck, cuffs and waist as well as lots of "ease" and flexibility. Garment designs for cold weather reverse the warm weather rules, to a great degree. Now the name of the game is to preserve body heat in as many "dead air" spaces as possible within the garment or layers of garments, to prevent cold air from penetrating the garment system and, at the same time, to keep the whole system dry.

## MOISTURE MANAGEMENT

The task of finding ways to assist the body in the management and control of its excess moisture production in warm conditions, during exercise or exertion by creating fabrics and materials that move the extra moisture away from the body in a controlled manner to be evaporated, keeping the wearer as cool and dry as possible.

# THE FOUR MAJOR

## INSULATION

The task of finding ways to prevent body heat from being lost or stolen from a clothing system by wind and cold through radiation, convection, conduction or evaporation in order to keep the wearer warm and cozy in even the harshest winter conditions or while doing the most strenuous activities.

The products and processes that have been developed to assist in the management of these processes are listed below. The Dictionary is organized for simplicity by grouping all of the products in the following categories:

## FIBERS:

The building blocks of nearly all of the products we will examine.

## INSULATION:

Approaches to trap and/or radiate back the body's own heat and keep it from being lost through conduction, convection, radiation and/or evaporation.

## MOISTURE MANAGEMENT:

Although primarily a concern in warmer conditions, this is very important in cold conditions when insulating clothing traps unwanted body heat, perspiration and water vapor during strenuous outdoor activities.

## WATERPROOF, WINDPROOF BUT BREATHABLE:

A year-round concern but most frequently addressed in cold, wet conditions. These fabric "systems" are relatively new and protect the wearer by maintaining dryness, wind resistance and still allow water vapor and excess heat to escape for dissipation and preventing the build-up of condensed moisture on the interior of the garment.

## STRETCH:

Stretch gives fabrics the ability to move and flex with the body's activity or it can help to mold the body itself. It also assists in making the wicking moisture management process work more efficiently as well as restrict unwanted muscle movement in repetitive exercise (compression).

**A**n additional category has been added to list the many other products and processes that are available to address a very broad range of performance needs that fall outside the moisture and heat regulation processes.

## SPECIAL PRODUCTS:

**W**e call these products "Other Miracles", and so they are. They range from anti-microbial/anti-fungal treatments, insect repelling fabrics, reflective fabrics for night safety, super tough fabrics that resist abrasion and tearing no matter how sharp the environment becomes, snake resistant fabrics and many more performance areas.

**E**ach section will begin with a discussion of each category, what they mean, how they work and the innovative approaches various trademark proprietors have taken to offer solutions to various problems associated with comfort and performance in an active world. Taken together, these segments will represent a good cross-section of the performance fibers, fabrics and finishes now in the marketplace to meet your active apparel needs.

## STRETCH

The task of adding some sort of stretchable or expandable (and recoverable) fiber or coating to a fabric structure or surface to allow it to support and shape parts of the body, to permit greater ease of movement, comfort and flexibility in active clothing, to provide body-hugging fit to clothing for style or function such as increasing efficiency and reducing fatigue.

## WATERPROOF, WINDPROOF BUT BREATHABLE

The task of creating some sort of barrier layer in a fabric or garment system that prevents rain, wind driven water and cold air from penetrating the garment's outer layers while allowing excess water vapor and excess trapped heat to escape, keeping the inner layers of clothing dry and warm and the wearer comfortable and dry in the worst of conditions.

# PERFORMANCE AREAS

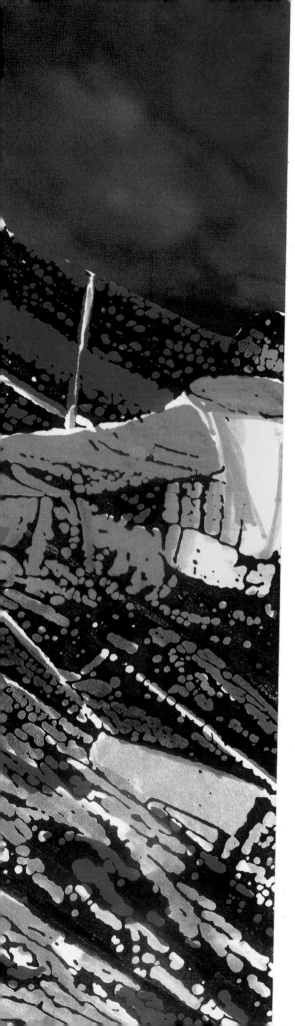

# FIBERS

## THE BUILDING BLOCKS OF PERFORMANCE

In order to understand the nature and characteristics of performance fabrics and garments, we must start with the building blocks that create the foundation and, in many cases, the whole reason for the existence of desired performance, appearance and care characteristics - the fibers they are made of.

In the beginning there were only natural fibers to help us achieve any kind of performance in apparel. They could be grouped into two major categories - protein or animal hair (or secretion, such as silk) and cellulosic or plant-derived materials (or sap, such as natural rubber). We'll call them "The Naturals".

## "THE NATURALS"

When discussing performance apparel with natural fibers, we are really talking about a very few of all the fibers and materials that exist in nature. Primarily, we are discussing wool, cotton, linen, silk and rubber. Briefly, let's examine each fiber, its use and reason to be considered to do the job in various aspects of active-wear performance.

# FIBERS

## "THE NATURALS"

### WOOL:

Wool is sometimes called the "perfect fiber" because of its wonderful properties. It is grown on a very wide variety of sheep in all parts of the world, each breed producing a very different and distinct type of wool fiber ranging from Merino wool with a fine, long staple (fiber length) hair that can be spun into fine, almost silk-like "worsted" yarns, to all sorts of short staple, coarse wool that can only be used for carpets and coarse blankets. Wool has a natural "crimp" that makes it "springy", resilient and an excellent insulator. It is very hydrophilic, allowing moisture to penetrate the fiber, and has a spongy core inside the fiber that picks up moisture and moves it in a controlled manner for evaporation while preventing the fiber from getting "chilled". (Wool will keep you warm even when it is wet, but it dries rather slowly, and it is naturally flame resistant.)

Wool fibers (like all hair fibers) are covered with "scales" that are all oriented in the same direction, like artichoke leaves. When an untreated wool fabric is washed vigorously in warm, soapy water, these scales can entangle themselves and compact the fabric (felting), causing a loss of dimension (not shrinkage). Today, there are excellent processes that allow wool to be machine washed without "shrinking" or, actually, felting. Wool is easily blended with other natural and synthetic staple fibers to create totally new performance-oriented fabrics.

With these properties, wool is still used in affordable, hard-wearing performance active-wear, especially in team sport jerseys and other apparel for soccer, rugby and ice hockey. Also, wool is still one of the most commonly used fibers for coats and performance outerwear as well as underwear for cold conditions and is the preferred fiber for many in sweaters and other insulating garments. Wool is still up there in the top performance fibers, natural or synthetic.

### COTTON:

Cotton is sometimes called "king cotton" because it is the most commonly used fiber in the world. Cotton is the seed hair of the cotton plant and is a fairly short staple fiber ranging from ¾" in length to a maximum of just over 2", as opposed to wool that can range from 1½" to 15". It is very hydrophilic (absorbs water) and has a hollow core in the center of the fiber that picks up moisture and transports it through the fiber for evaporation. Cotton is easily blended with synthetic fibers to enhance its unwanted natural properties, such as a tendency to wrinkle and to shrink in washing. (It should be noted that 100% cotton fabrics and garments can be shrinkage-controlled through pre-shrinkage, compaction, Sanforizing®, etc., or by resin treatments in finishing. Cotton is one of the heaviest of all the fibers, is easily saturated with perspiration in heavy exercise and dries rather slowly compared to synthetic fibers. In spite of this, cotton is still the fiber of choice

for most warmer weather or indoor activities because of its absorbency, comfort, affordability and general easy care.

Nothing has to be said about cotton's uses. It was and is still the most commonly used of all fibers in activewear, in spite of some drawbacks. It is economical, flexible in its applications (knits, wovens, brushed fabrics, ribs, etc.) and generally comfortable and a good value for most uses.

## SILK:

Nature's own continuous filament fiber, silk is the product of a silkworm and mulberry leaves. (Raw silk involves oak leaves, but it is hardly ever used in active apparel.) The silkworm creates a double strand, continuous filament (no breaks) that is about 3000 yards long to form its cocoon. Silk is VERY fine, very strong for its weight (as strong as steel, by weight), absorbent and has very good insulating properties. Also, it is easy to dye in brilliant colors and can be woven or knitted into very light-weight fabrics. Silk has been used for insulating underwear for extreme conditions where warmth without weight is important. Although quite expensive, silk is still a desired product for performance underwear and outerwear around the world. Of course, rayon and nylon were specifically designed to imitate silk and, in fact, the terms "microdenier" or "microfiber" refer to synthetic fibers that have filaments that are finer than a single strand of silk.

Today, silk is combined with microfibers to create very light-weight fabrics that are used in windbreakers, tops and light weather rainwear.

## LINEN:

The oldest fiber used by man after he got out of his "animal skin" phase, linen can be traced back before 10,000 BC and was the fiber used to wrap the mummies, not cotton. (Cotton is a "baby" by comparison, having its origin in India about 3,500 BC.) Derived from the stalk of a flax plant, linen has a staple length of 10" to 20". This makes it easy to spin, but the fiber is quite brittle and the fabrics made of it are brittle and wrinkle easily. In fact, if a crease is repeated in the same place in the linen cloth, it can break and fall apart. Historically, linen was the summer fabric of choice for many warm weather activities, such as tennis and golf. However, today, the days of white linens on the tennis court and the 18th green are long gone. Cotton and synthetic fibers have won this one!

## NATURAL RUBBER:

The living sap of the rubber tree, latex rubber is a manufactured fiber that was commercialized by Goodyear in the 1920's. Rubber was first used in performance apparel as galoshes (rubber boots) and as a coating for fabric used in other rainwear products. When rubber yarns were developed, they were incorporated in several activewear products ranging from swimwear, foundation fabrics, support garments and body appliances of all sorts as well as for waistbands, wraps and support bandages, among other uses.

Latex rubber is still the fiber of choice in several products destined for the performance market, especially in hosiery tops, some specialized control garments, support wraps and waist- bands. (These yarns are usually covered with other fibers for protection and durability.) Of course, in today's world, a "new" synthetic elastic fiber, spandex, has created a revolution in stretch apparel, and we will address that revolution in a separate section called "STRETCH".

## "THE MIRACLE FIBERS"

Although there are a large number of synthetic, "miracle" fibers available today, we will focus on the most common fibers used for performance wear. They are nylon (polyamide), polyester, acrylic, olefin (polypropylene or polyolefin), acetate and spandex. Let's get to know them.

The category of synthetic fibers we want to examine are created from sets of long chain molecules, called polymers (these are the same base as plastics), and are all derived from petroleum-based chemical by-products by distilling crude oil. (Rayon, acetate and triacetate fibers, the other synthetic category, are derived from wood pulp or cellulose.) All of these fibers are created in continuous filament form, like silk, and, in most cases, are knitted or woven in that form. However, acrylic fiber is always

chopped up into staple lengths for spinning into acrylic yarns, as are certain amounts of polyester and polypropylene so they may be used to blend with other natural and synthetic staple fibers in spinning.

## NYLON (Polyamide):

Although rayon and acetate were the first synthetic fibers to be commercialized (discovered in 1928 and commercialized by DuPont in 1940), nylon was the first real "miracle fiber". Stronger than steel and as fine as silk, nylon became the prototype of all oil-based synthetic fibers in performance wear. Nylon is hard wearing, weather resistant (although weakened by ultraviolet light), easily dyeable and cleanable and able to be thermoset (heated near melting, positioned in the shape desired and cooled, retaining that form permanently) to reduce shrinkage and retain its shape forever. Nylon reigned supreme for many years as the fiber of choice for garment shell fabrics, lingerie, swimwear, linings, knit shirting fabrics, hosiery, luggage and bags, tents, skiwear, etc. Today, nylon still is the key outer shell performance fiber and the most common synthetic fiber to be "married" with spandex for a wide variety of performance apparel.

## POLYESTER:

Born in England in 1950, like nylon, polyester, is an oil-based fiber created by "melt spinning", whereby the ingredients are combined under great heat in molten state to form a polymer that is extruded through a "spinneret" or shower head-type device to form a yarn. Polyester proved itself a somewhat more flexible fiber than nylon. For example, polyester could be heat set (thermoset) at a variety of temperatures, allowing it to be processed in several steps before ending up in a particular form. (Nylon only allows you to heat set it once and never again.) For instance, you could produce a heat set fabric (heat set to reduce or remove shrinkage and wrinkling), make a pair of pants from the fabric and then heat set the fabric again in garment form to create a crease that would never wash or iron out.

Polyester is difficult to dye, but, once the color is put into the fiber, it is very durable to most washing and wearing conditions. Also, the performance characteristics of polyester can be more easily modified than nylon with various performance-enhancing treatments and processes when it is being "extruded" or, later, in yarn form or in fabric finishing. A good example would be the addition of a "wicking" agent that would change a normally hydrophobic fiber with little or no moisture management characteristics into a first class wicking fiber, capable of moving large quantities of moisture away from the body for evaporation. Today, polyester is the most popular performance fiber in the industry because of its flexibility and variety of aesthetics, durability and performance.

## OLEFIN (Polypropylene, polyolefin) :

Born in 1960, this thermoplastic fiber spent many years having little luck finding a home in the apparel market. However, it did meet with success in other markets because of its many unusual properties, such as being lighter than water (it floats! - good for boat lines and nautical rope), totally weather and rot-proof (great for Astroturf and outdoor furniture or umbrellas), vermin-proof (bugs and varmints hate it! - good for life vests, packaging, etc.) and is impossible to dye, except when the color is added to the fiber in molten state. (It is totally colorfast, even in sunlight - great for outdoor furniture, carpets and auto fabrics.)

The first major apparel success was in ski underwear where another characteristic of this "different" fiber was used - it transports moisture very well. Also, the fabrics made from it are very light in weight and stay that way, no matter how hard you exercise and perspire. In addition, olefin has quite a low thermal conductivity, helping to keep body heat from escaping from the garment system through conduction. Working off these advantages, performance fabric and activewear designers have adopted olefin as their special performance "miracle fiber" and are finding more and more uses for it used alone or in combination with other fibers and finishes.

## ACETATE:

A cellulosic fiber made from wood

pulp and special chemicals that allow the wood pulp to be drawn into a fiber. Acetate is the "first cousin" of rayon, being made from similar materials and having many similar properties. They differ in some ways as well, including the fact that acetate is produced in continuous filament form while rayon is usually cut into staple form and spun into fiber. Similarities include a warm, friendly "hand", excellent absorbency (and resulting excellent dyeing and printing characteristics) and wearing comfort. It is a soft fiber and does not have a very good abrasion resistance and durability. It can be made to have anti-microbial performance built in.

## ACRYLIC:

Acrylic fibers have been with us since the 50's and were originally developed to be the synthetic substitute for wool. Extensively used in sweaters (athletic and dress), hosiery, warm-ups, carpets, blankets, brushed linings, children's wear and other warm wear apparel, acrylic fibers have enjoyed great acceptance in the performance wear market. Always used in staple, spun yarn form, acrylics are among the strongest fibers made. They are easily textured and bulked to trap heat and are commonly brushed in their applications for heat retention. They dye beautifully and are reputed to assist in moisture management. Microdenier acrylics are now available and new anti-microbial

features are being built into some to prevent the growth of odor- causing bacteria, mold and mildew from growing on the fabrics. Also, it is now easy to print on acrylic fabrics and garments. Acrylic fibers have earned and hold an important place in the performance actionwear industry. Although they have had a reputation for "pilling", the newer versions of the fiber (low pill acetate and microdenier versions) have found ways to control the problem successfully.

## SPANDEX

Man's "knock-off" of rubber was the brainchild of DuPont and came into the market in the 60's. However, it had to wait until the 90's to achieve its current success and realize its promise. In fact, spandex created the "Great Stretch Revolution" that we will address in a separate section in the book. Check it out.

Indeed, fibers are the building blocks of every product in this book and tend to dictate the performance of most of the products that will follow in this book. Let us introduce you to the world of branded performance fibers and their makers, and, more importantly, to the wonderful things they do that make today's performance apparel and products work, look and feel better than ever before.

# FIBERS

## ACRILAN®

**Monsanto's** well known trademark for their acrylic fiber collection. Acrylic is a fiber that was originally designed to simulate wool and, through the years, it has found all sorts of end uses in performance apparel ranging from bulky sweaters and warm fleeces to athletic socks and tough outerwear. Quite light for its bulk, easily dyeable and now readily printable, acrylics are very strong and durable fibers. Also, acrylic fibers are touted to be good "moisture managers". **Acrilan®**, like all other acrylic fibers, is bi-polar (having a positive charge on one end of the molecule and a negative charge on the other end) and interacts with water molecules (which are bi-polar as well). This electrical interaction between the water and the fiber is reputed to 'excite' the water molecules and keep them from maintaining their very strong attraction to each other, creating the powerful surface tension that keeps water in droplet form. Much of the moisture remains in water vapor form, thus allowing an easy vapor transport of moisture through the fabric and promotes the wicking of the liquid water remaining.

## ALPHA™ OLEFIN

**Amoco Fabrics & Fibers Company** presents its spun olefin (polypropylene or polyolefin) fiber, a 'second generation' fiber that offers superior performance features including better heat resistance, bulk and dry cleanability. **Alpha™ Olefin's** performance features include moisture management that transfers moisture away from the body by moving it along and around the fibers to the exterior of the garment or to another fabric layer for efficient evaporation. Also, because of the fiber's low specific gravity and low thermal conductivity, it helps to retain body heat and offers great bulk for insulation with little weight. With greater heat resistance and durability than other polypropylene fibers, Alpha could be the pick of the olefin crop for anything from underwear to outerwear.

## CAPROLAN® NYLON

**Allied Signal's** brand name for their basic type .66 nylon fiber that is commonly used in performance active apparel, generally as a shell fabric because of its great strength and abrasion resistance. It is relatively lightweight, easy to care, fast drying and can be dyed in vertually any color. Easily found in skiwear, team jackets, active/outerwear, rainwear, snowboarding garments and innerwear.

## CAPTIMA® NYLON

If you are looking for a "spun hand" in a continuous filament synthetic fiber, you should look for fabrics made from **Allied Signal's Captima®** nylon yarn. The yarn is air-jet textured to raise the surface filaments of the fiber, making it feel 'fuzzy' and cotton or wool-like. Extremely durable, lightweight and easily dyeable, Captima® is used in hunting clothes, surfwear and other sportswear apparel.

# FIBERS

## CAPTIVA® NYLON

Found primarily in knitted constructions (but also in wovens), **Captiva®** nylon is a high filament count continuous filament yarn from **Allied Signal** that has a soft, silky, buttery hand, yet is very durable and easy care. Easily dyeable in bright, rich colors, Captiva® is a great fiber for running wear and aerobic clothes, intimate apparel, as well as other types of activewear.

## COMFORTREL®

**ComFortrel®** is a special moisture management and 'breathable' polyester fiber from **Wellman, Inc.** where the performance characteristics are built into the fiber itself. (This is termed as "inherent", or "by its nature", or as a property of the fiber itself.) A special chemistry is added to the fiber when it is being extruded that allows it to easily wick moisture away from the body and contribute to the moisture management and "breathability" of the end use product. Either used as a fine denier continuous filament or as a staple fiber for blending with other synthetics or natural fibers, ComFortrel® can be easily napped or brushed to improve its hand or insulating properties and yet maintain its appearance wash after wash. Look for the tags and labels on knitted apparel and underwear for activewear.

## COOLMAX®

**Coolmax®** is **DuPont's** trademark for a broad range of high-performance, tested and certified fabrics that are made from their patented tetra-channeled cross section (4 channels) polyester fibers by licensed fabric and garment manufacturers. The fiber involved has a cross section that looks somewhat like a very pregnant figure "8" with a slightly larger third lobe positioned between the two end lobes. This configuration creates four channels that run the length of the fiber and very efficiently carry away the body's perspiration for evaporation. With moisture management features built into the fibers when they are made, there is no "topical" or finish treatment to wash or wear off. Also, Coolmax® dries very quickly, keeping the wearer comfortable and performing efficiently. Activewear, aerobicwear, placket shirts, casual tops, T's, fleeces, socks and a lot more are all available carrying the Coolmax® tags.

## CORDURA® PLUS

**Cordura® Plus** combines the toughness for which **Cordura®** is known, but with a soft hand. This is an air-jet textured, high tenacity (tough to break) nylon fiber that has superior abrasion resistance and, in shell fabric applications, woven into tight structures, it is quite water and wind resistant. Available in a variety of weights, you'll find this tough guy from **DuPont** in activewear, climbing gear, hunting gear and other demanding apparel applications.

## CYSTAR® AF

**Sterling Fibers** presents a new acrylic fiber with anti-microbial protection and performance built in. Called

# FIBERS

**Cystar® AF**, it is the only anti-microbial acrylic fiber produced in the USA and protects garments against the development of a broad spectrum of bacteria, fungi and yeast that can cause odors and mildew growth in active apparel. Available in activewear, intimate apparel and hosiery, Cystar® AF offers long-lasting protection because the anti-microbial agent is spun into the fiber when it is made and cannot wash or wear off.

## DORLASTAN® SPANDEX

**Bayer Corporation**, one of Europe's chemical manufacturing giants, has recently begun American production of their internationally known spandex fiber, **Dorlastan®**, offering a wide range of elastomeric (stretch) fibers to the performance stretch apparel markets as well as to the fashion and apparel industries in the United States. Dorlastan® is now available in a broad variety of circular knitted, warp knitted and, soon, woven fabric applications for all sorts of activewear and performance outerwear and underwear garments. Spandex adds a special elastic comfort, fit and control factor to most clothing and can be needed for top performance by the serious competitor.

## DRALON® ACRYLIC

**Dralon®** acrylic adds its international reputation as a premium acrylic fiber from **Bayer Corporation** (yes, they are the aspirin people as well) to the acrylic rebirth in the American market. They offer new generation acrylic fibers that are pill resistant, available

in wonderfully soft and luxurious microfibers and come in all kinds of beautiful, wash-fast colors. Dralon® acrylic fibers, as all other acrylic fibers, were originally designed to simulate natural wool fibers and, today, they are just beginning to realize their potential. Even the built-in bi-polar character of acrylic fibers is supposed to assist in efficient moisture management in activewear without additional treatments to the fabrics. Look for Dralon® acrylic in sweaters, socks and other performance and leisure apparel.

## DURASPUN®

The performance fiber champion for athletic socks - **Duraspun®** high bulk acrylic fibers from **Monsanto**. Tough as nails and as soft as down, Duraspun® fibers also bring the comfort of superior moisture management and high bulk resilience to sport, dress and athletic socks, but especially to athletic socks that really take a beating. Acrylic fiber is among the strongest fibers made and special patented spinning conditions at Monsanto just enhance this remarkable fiber that much more. The **"Smart Yarn®"** of choice in hosiery is Duraspun® acrylic.

## ECLIPSE® NYLON

Nylon is tough stuff! In fact, by weight, it is stronger than steel! But nylon has an "Achilles heel" - ultraviolet light (U.V.). With prolonged exposure to sunlight (that contains ultraviolet light as well as the "visual" light spectrum), nylon will lose its strength

29

and fall apart or turn to powder. (Maybe you have seen some old flags go to tatters after being out in the sun too long?) Now, **Allied Signal** has been the first to develop **Eclipse®** nylon that is specially formulated to be extremely U.V. resistant even after long sunlight exposure and repeated abrasion and washings. Obviously, it is ideal for all swimwear, beachwear garments and sailing gear. (To say nothing of flags!) So, quit worrying about your bathing suit or windbreaker falling apart in public if it's made of Eclipse®.

## ESP®

If "affordable comfort stretch" is desired in a woven or knitted fabric, it is possible that **Trevira's ESP (Extra Stretch Performance)** textured filament polyester will fill the bill. Created from a special polymer, this polyester fiber is specially textured with a high degree of crimp that allows the yarn to have a relatively high degree of elasticity and recovery. (This is a very different approach to stretch and elasticity than spandex which has greatly more elasticity and stretch and has a much stronger "modulus" or recovery power.) ESP® is commonly used as a filling yarn in woven fabrics (such as denims) providing one-way comfort stretch and recovery or is used in knitted fabrics to produce two-way stretch. It can be found in a broad range of active apparel ranging from swimwear to jeans, cycling wear, tights, fashion, and other bottom weights.

## FORTREL®

**Fortrel®** is **Wellman, Inc.**'s trademark for their broad family of polyester fibers. This trademark is over 30 years old and one of the best known and respected trademarks in the textile industry, representing quality polyester fibers for all sorts of apparel, home furnishings and industrial applications, including a very broad range of performance apparel and accessory end use products related to activewear, actionwear and team sports.

## FORTREL® ECOSPUN®

One of the first synthetic fiber collections made 100% from post-consumer recycled polyester containers, **Wellman's Fortrel® Ecospun®** polyester fibers are claimed to keep 2.4 billion plastic containers out of landfills every year while saving 650,000 barrels of oil annually as well as other environment-conscious benefits. The recycled, environmentally friendly polyester is used exactly like any other polyester and can be found in a very wide range of top quality, high performance fabrics and garments for the active market.

## FORTREL® MICROSPUN®

Among the "finest of the fine" in Fortrel® polyester fibers, **Wellman's Fortrel® MicroSpun®** products create a wide range of soft, luxurious-feeling microfiber fabrics for the activewear and performance wear industry. Finer than silk, these microdenier, continuous filament fibers hide their performance and toughness in a soft hand, but they are "champs" when it comes to wrinkle and pill resistance, easy care, durability and comfort. They are much more than just a pretty face - and hand.

## GLOSPAN®

**Glospan®** is **Globe Manufacturing Company's** trademark for their family of spandex elastomeric fibers that add wonderful ease and stretchable comfort to all types of apparel as well as the power and control that is necessary for shape retention and muscle control in repetitive exercise. Generally, there are two types of spandex fibers, and Globe makes both. One type is polyester-based and is used primarily for heavier denier (coarser) applications such as elastic for hosiery tops, bandages, waistbands, etc. The other type is polyether-based and is produced in finer deniers. It is the type of spandex commonly used for sportswear, swimwear, foundation garments and most active apparel applications. Globe Manufacturing is a total elastic fiber source, offering a broad range of natural rubber (latex) yarns, both types of spandex fibers and a clear, see-through spandex fiber for sheer hosiery.

## HYDROFIL® NYLON

**Allied Signal** has developed this inherently water-loving (hydrophilic) nylon fiber designed especially for the activewear, performance activewear and team sports markets. The fiber has a hydrophilic substance built into

the fiber when it is made so it will never wash out or wear off for the life of the garment. Designed to rapidly wick or transport moisture away from the body, the fiber is commonly used in conjunction with another hydrophobic (water hating) fiber, but wickable, like brushed or napped polyester yarn, that is woven or knitted to be next to the skin with the **Hydrofil®** nylon used on the outer side of the fabric. The wickable polyester picks up the body moisture and transports it to the Hydrofil® layer for rapid evaporation. This "pumping" system for the perspiration is called a "push/pull" moisture control and works very well to keep the wearer warm and dry, preventing that 'clammy' feeling after exertion.

## INNOVA® POLYOLEFIN

It has been said that a person's perception of warmth and performance in thermal wear is a garment that stays dry and retains body heat. Thermal wear made of **Innova®** continuous filament polyolefin from **Amoco Fabrics & Fibers Co.** certainly passes those tests. Employing polyolefin's (aka: polypropylene or olefin) natural hydrophobic nature and its excellent water transfer characteristics (wicking), combined with the fiber's low thermal conductivity rate that helps retain the body's heat, Innova® keeps the warmth where you want it while moving moisture away from you. Used by itself in a brushed fabric, as a body contact layer component in a fabric system or even as swimwear or divewear (it's quick drying, anti-microbial with no worry about bacteria or mildew and chlorine won't affect it), Innova® could be the fiber of choice for a broad array of performance activewear.

## LYCRA® SPANDEX

**DuPont** introduced spandex elastomeric fiber in 1958 and they named it **Lycra®** the following year. Introduced as a substitute for natural rubber (latex), it can be said that spandex revolutionized the stretch fabric industry and had an enormous impact on the activewear, foundations, swimwear and performance wear industries, making new levels of comfort and performance possible. With up to 700% stretch and complete recovery, Lycra® is the most commonly identified brand related to spandex fibers internationally. In order to apply the trademark to products containing the fiber, it is necessary for the fabric manufacturer to be licensed by DuPont and for their fabrics to meet established certification standards set forth by DuPont. From basic body hugging comfort to power compression performance, Lycra® can be found in all sorts of apparel ranging from silky high fashion to rugged mountain climbing gear.

## MICROMATTIQUE™

**DuPont's** special trademark for its family of premium microdenier fibers intended for activewear, active sportswear and athleisure. (Looking active,

looking good, sweating not!) Wonderfully soft and luxurious to the touch, these fibers are easily textured or 'face-finished' to give a chamois or sueded texture. Also, because of their fineness, **Micromattique™** microfibers offer great coverage for the weight of yarn used in the fabric and, like all microfibers, with special constructions and finishes, they can offer good water and wind resistance without weight. But, mostly, they just feel GREAT!

## MICROMATTIQUE™ MX

A new approach to microdenier yarn technology that combines the aesthetic attributes of microfibers with the strength, body and resilience of standard fine denier fibers (2 denier per filament as opposed to .5 denier per filament in microdenier fibers). Leave it to **DuPont** to offer **Micromattique™ MX** that combines both filament weights when the yarn is made. As an example, out of 200 total filaments in the yarn, only 24 are the heavier denier, but the heavier fibers make up about 1/3 of the total yarn weight. Result? More body and bounce to the fabrics, a spun-like hand, more flexible fabric styling and a fine heather effect when dyed.

## MICROMATTIQUE™ XF

As if the original **Micromattique™** microdenier fibers were not fine enough, **DuPont** now offers **Micromattique™ XF** (extra fine). Only 1/3 the size of silk filaments, this ultimate microfiber allows woven, circular knit and tricot fabric manufacturers to create fabrics of unparalleled luxury, with a "face powder" touch, superior softness, drape and comfort. Easily textured and face finished, when used in tight fabric constructions, these fibers are water and wind resistant, ideal for golf tops, rainwear and other medium to lighter weight performance outerwear.

## MICROSAFE® ACETATE

A special acetate fiber (acetate is a close relative to rayon protection) designed by **Celanese Acetate** with anti-microbial protection that provides continuous, built-in control of the spread of bacteria, fungi, mold, mildew and yeast. Acetate is a very absorbent fiber with an open pore structure that allows easy migration of moisture and prints and dyes easily. **MicroSafe®** is usually combined with other fibers in underwear, socks and shoes where warm, damp conditions can invite bacterial growth and mildew.

## MICROSELECT™

**Microselect™** is **DuPont's** special microdenier polyester fiber especially designed for the activewear market. With a combination of hollow and "C"- shaped hollow core cross section (like cotton's cross section profile), the fabrics made from these yarns have the aesthetics with the hand of silk and cotton, but all the performance goodies of polyester. Specially designed to transport moisture away from the body (wicking) in next-to-body clothing, the fiber is also claimed to have superior effectiveness as a

wind barrier and as insulation. The **Microselect™** trademark is licensed to fabric mills upon complying with special fabric standards established and tested by DuPont.

## MICROSUPPLEX™

**MicroSupplex™** is **DuPont's** trademark for its nylon microfiber offering heightened cottony-soft aesthetics with enhanced function. Designed for apparel that demands high performance fabrics, MicroSupplex™can be found in all types of clothing, from raincoats to running shorts. In woven applications, it allows for tighter, more densely constructed fabrics that have twice the wind resistance, water resistance and abrasion resistance as standard nylon fabrics.

## MICROSUPREME® ACRYLIC

Taking a new generation of acrylic fibers into a new generation of performance applications, **Sterling Fibers'** **Microsupreme®** fibers are micro-fine (.9 denier per filament) , lightweight and comfortable for all sorts of active apparel. It is claimed that because of the acrylic fiber's built-in electrostatic bi-polar charge, water (which is also bi-polar) tends to react with the acrylic fibers to keep a lot of perspiration in vapor form to easily move through the fabric structure and dissipate in the air while the liquid water is easily "wicked away". Both moisture and water vapor move from the body to the exterior of the garment for further absorption by another, more absorbent garment layer or to the fabric "skin" for evaporation. Supposedly, the fabric does not have to be in direct contact with the body to handle the water vapor phase. Ideal for thermal underwear and other active intimate apparel, hosiery, skiwear, and actionwear.

## P.C.R.®

**P.C.R.®** is **Patagonia's** trademark that stands for "Post Consumer Recycled" or fiber (polyester) that has been recycled from previously used, salvaged and reused soft drink bottles. Wellman, Inc. is the fiber source and they identify these yarns as **EcoSpun®** fibers. Patagonia is using these yarns in a very broad range of their fabrications for all sorts of end uses. Look for the "P.C.R.®" logo on the Patagonia clothes made from these recycled materials.

## PROSPIN®

**Cone Mills** has created a fresh approach to achieve a performance cotton yarn that keeps all the good news about cotton without some of the bad news, like shrinkage, wrinkling and only modest strength. By taking a long staple pima cotton (long staple American grown cotton) fiber blend and spinning it around a synthetic continuous filament polyester core (using a special patented spinning system), they have created **ProSpin®** yarn. The performance of this hybrid yarn in fabrics include increased strength (3 times regular cotton), wrinkle resistance (heat-settable into a crease without weakening resins that need "curing"- in the crease) and

shrink resistance. At the same time, the fabrics feel and look like cotton and absorb moisture easily for comfort. Now available in a wide range of woven fabrics for shorts, pants, jacket shells and shirts for activewear.

## SALUS®

Take all the virtues of polypropylene (alias - olefin; alias - polyolefin) fibers (lightweight, chemically inert, high moisture transport characteristics, static resistance, no absorbency, colorfastness, low radiant heat transport) and amplify one of them - the fiber's mold and bacterial resistance - to become actually anti-microbial and you have **Filament Fiber Technology's Salus®** polypropylene fiber. The anti-microbial protection is permanently incorporated in the fiber during the extrusion process and will never wear or wash out for the life of the fiber or garment. Definitely an excellent choice for swimwear, aerobics, wet suits, thermal underwear, shoe liners, socks, etc.

## SPORTOUCH® NYLON

A true microfiber nylon yarn (finer than silk) from **BASF** is offers a rich, silk-like hand and luster to both stretch and non-stretch activewear and active sportswear end uses. **SporTouch®** nylon adds a creamy, soft feel, comfort and fit to performance fabrics for the active world.

## SUPPLEX®

Who says nylon must feel slick to act like a synthetic fiber? **Supplex®** nylon fabrics are trying to put an end to

that myth!  Made with special ultra-fine filaments that have been specially air-jet textured to add a "fuzzy" and friendly 'hand', when properly made into fabrics, Supplex® has a very cottony feel and appearance that is permanent, wash after wash. **DuPont** claims that the fabrics are up to 36% softer than other nylon fabrics and blends and are reputed to be water and wind resistant, breathable, strong as well as being cottony soft. A natural to be blended with **Lycra®** spandex, it is also claimed to be fast drying for added comfort in activewear and odor free. There is a certification program involved, so contact DuPont before you use the trademark. Look for all sorts of activewear and performance clothes where you would expect to find cotton and that's where you can find Supplex®.

## TACTEL® NYLON

**DuPont's** family of **Tactel®** nylon yarns allows innovative fabric creation for performance outerwear, activewear, exercise wear and performance casualwear. Tactel®, either flat or false twist textured, has great aesthetics and superior nylon performance. In tightly woven shell fabrics for skiing or mountain climbing, Tactel® is water and wind resistant, yet breathable. Performance knits in Tactel® have a soft, smooth appearance, can be dyed in rich colors and have a luxurious hand.

## TELAR®

**Filament Fiber Technology, Inc.**

is the producer of these branded **Telar®** polypropylene (alias - olefin; alias - polyolefin) fibers and yarns. The difference is that these fibers are available in a wonderful palate of colors that are built into the fibers as they are being created. Because polypropylene is TOTALLY hydrophobic (water hating), there is no way to put color into or on to the fiber after it is created, so the color must be put into the fiber when it is molten or "in solution" - hence the term "solution dyed". Such colors are permanent and never wash out or fade. The fibers are also the lightest fibers made. Their unique crystalline structure transports moisture in vapor phase, keeping the skin dry at all times. Since it is hydrophobic, it resists the growth of mold, mildew and bacteria. This classification of fibers, in any form, has the lowest thermal conductivity of any fiber, making it warmer in the winter and cooler in the summer. A remarkable fiber, indeed, for underwear, fleeces, swimwear, wet suits, aerobics, active stretch fabrics, etc.

## TENCEL®

The newest major apparel fiber under the sun!  And it is made from 100% natural cellulose (wood pulp) in a non-toxic, more environmentally friendly manner than most fibers. **Tencel®** is the brain-child of **Courtaulds Fibers, Inc.** and far out performs any other cellulose-based fibers, such as acetate and rayon, in terms of strength (wet or dry) and is more absorbent than cotton. Made using a solvent spinning process where nearly all of the solvent used in the process is recycled (the fiber's generic name is **LYOCELL®** ), the fiber is claimed to "breathe"(absorb). Easily dyeable into deep, rich colors that are washable in most shades and printable, Tencel® has a good natural luster and is finding a home in men's and women's apparel and actionwear.

## THERMASTAT®

Here is another engineered performance fiber from **DuPont** that offers both superior insulation in basic fabrics (not a fiberfill, but an insulating fiber) as well as excellent moisture management. **ThermaStat®** is a specially licensed trademark controlled by DuPont and can only be applied to products made by licensed manufacturers that have been tested against strict standards and approved by DuPont's lab. The fiber that makes the products perform so well is made from specially treated **Dacron®** polyester polymers that encourage wicking for moisture management and fast drying. At the same time, a hollow core in each fiber traps warm air for improved insulation. In fact, DuPont claims that the ThermaStat® certified fabrics dry 20% faster than competitive products and 50% faster than cotton - and stay warmer in the process. Thermals, jacket lining, hosiery, ski turtlenecks and tops are among the applications.

## TREVIRA® FINESSE® MICROFIBER

This is an ultra-fine **Trevira®** microfiber polyester group from Trevira with denier weights of nearly ½ denier per filament and slightly heavier. This fineness allows high density weaving or knitting to create shell fabrics that are featherweight, so densely constructed that they will not allow wind and rain to penetrate the pores of the woven structure, yet large enough to allow body moisture vapor to escape and evaporate (breathe). This is accomplished without coatings, membranes or other finishes that can add bulk and weight to a fabric. **Trevira® Finesse®** remains soft, pliable and lightweight, ideal for windbreaker jackets, tops, running gear, jogging clothes and other activewear end uses.

## TREVIRA® MICRO FILAMENT

**Trevira** offers their version of polyester microfibers, branded **Trevira® Micro Filament** . This is a broadly based trademark designed to cover a broad range of polyester fibers where every filament (strand) within the total yarn bundle is finer than 1 denier per filament, generally regarded to be the average fineness of natural silk fibers. The great advantages of such fibers in fabrics are greater softness and drapability, ease of face finishing, greater natural wickability, greater coverage and the ability to be knitted into very fine (silky) or tightly knitted fabric structures that are wind and water resistant without further finishes being added. And, all of them are easy care fibers and wrinkle resistant.

# FIBERS

## TREVIRA® MICRONESSE®

If you want to create ultra-fine yarns for lightweight outerwear shell fabrics to be used alone or blended with other fibers, **Trevira® Micronesse®** continuous filament microdenier polyester fibers from **Trevira®** could answer your need. Easy care, wrinkle resistant, lightweight and colorfast, fabrics made from these fibers have a beautiful drape, are easily sueded for the "peach skin" 'hand' or fully napped for a fleece or pile fabric effect and are hard wearing. For tops, windbreakers, warm-ups, light shells and golf jackets, Micronesse® fibers are out there for you.

## TREVIRA® MICROTHERM™

If you are thinking of creating an energy efficient lining fabric or a knitted fabric that has breathable, moisture management properties, perhaps you might want to consider **Trevira® Microtherm™** polyester fiber from **Trevira®**. Aside from the fiber's microdenier (finer than silk) character, the improved wicking and breathability, this fiber is reputed to be warmer than conventional linings because of its low thermal conductivity. Conductivity is one of the three ways the body loses heat (the others are convection and radiation) and the slower the conductivity of body heat, the warmer the individual will remain. Of course, the microfiber character of the yarns makes it easy to nap or brush to achieve a raised fabric face ranging from a peach-skin suede to a dense pile and the resulting warmth retention advantage of a face finished lining or outer shell.

## ULTRA TOUCH™ NYLON

With its expertise in the high filament yarn category, **BASF** has created an affordable family of fine dpf (denier per filament) yarns to bring ultra softness, smoothness and comfort to the stretch intimate apparel and activewear markets. Available in bright and dull lusters and in a variety of deniers, **Ultra Touch™** nylon permits styling diversity in the "feel-good" fabric category.

## ZEFSPORT® NYLON

This **BASF** product is highly uniform Type 6 nylon fiber that takes color beautifully and is available in both bright and dull lusters for maximum styling flexibility. It marries well with spandex fibers to make some of the market's superior tricot stretch fabrics for swimwear and activewear featuring wonderful fit and comfort.

# FIBERS GROUPED BY CHEMICAL TYPE

## NYLON
CAPROLAN ............. ALLIED SIGNAL
CAPTIMA ................ ALLIED SIGNAL
CAPTIVA ................. ALLIED SIGNAL
CORDURA PLUS .............. DUPONT
ECLIPSE ................. ALLIED SIGNAL
HYDROFIL .............. ALLIED SIGNAL
HYDROFIL II ........... ALLIED SIGNAL
MICROSUPPLEX .............. DUPONT
SPORTOUCH NYLON ............. BASF
SUPPLEX ........................ DUPONT
TACTEL ........................... DUPONT
ULTRA TOUCH ...................... BASF
ZEFSPORT ............................ BASF

## POLYESTER
COMFORTREL ................ WELLMAN
COOLMAX ...................... DUPONT
ESP ................................. TREVIRA
FORTREL ...................... WELLMAN
FORTREL ECOSPUN ....... WELLMAN
FORTREL MICROSPUN .... WELLMAN
MICROMATTIQUE ........... DUPONT
MICROMATTIQUE MX ....... DUPONT
MICROMATTIQUE XF ........ DUPONT
MICROSELECT .................. DUPONT
P.C.R. .......................... PATAGONIA
PROSPIN ................. NORTH POINT
SPTSWR. (CONE)
THERMASTAT .................. DUPONT
TREVIRA ........................... TREVIRA
TREVIRA MICROFILAMENT . TREVIRA
TREVIRA MICRONESSE ...... TREVIRA
TREVIRA MICROTHERM ..... TREVIRA

## POLYPROPYLENE/ OLEFIN
ALPHA OLEFIN .................. AMOCO
FABRICS & FIBERS
ALPHA PILE ....................... AMOCO
FABRICS & FIBERS
INNOVA ............................ AMOCO
FABRICS & FIBERS
SALUS ........................... .FILAMENT
FIBER TECHNOLOGIES
TELAR ........................... .FILAMENT
FIBER TECHNOLOGIES

## ACRYLIC
ACRILAN ..................... MONSANTO
CYSTAR AF ..................... STERLING
DRALON ................... BAYER CORP.
DURASPUN ................ MONSANTO
MICROSUPREME .. STERLING FIBERS

## SPANDEX
DORLASTAN .............. BAYER CORP.
GLOSPAN ........... GLOBE MFG. CO.
LYCRA .............................. DUPONT

## CELLULOSE
TENCEL (LYOCELL) .... COURTAULDS

## ACETATE
CELANESE ACETATE ....... CELANESE
MICROSAFE .................. CELANESE

FIBERS

# PROTECTING YOUR OWN HEAT SOURCE

Insulation in apparel of any kind is finding ways to keep the body's own heat from being lost through:

## Radiation
## Convection
## Conduction
## Evaporation

# INSULATION

## RETAINING YOUR OWN BODY HEAT TO STAY WARM

**Heat is lost through:**
> **Radiation**
> **Convection**
> **Conduction**
> **Evaporation**

Conduction and Convection are the most common "heat eaters" in activewear.

■ **To protect against convection heat loss,** check your clothing design and snug-up the hood, cuffs, placket front, the waist, hip and ankle areas of your clothing and wear warm accessories and undergarments.

■ **To protect against conduction heat loss,** check your selection of a wide variety of products in this Dictionary especially designed to reduce such heat loss, from fiberfills, thermal fabrics, napped pile fabrics and sliver knits to special fabrics treated with space age phase-change coatings. Also,

certain fibers have slower rates of heat conduction (such as polypropylene) that can help retain heat.

■ **To protect against radiation heat loss,** look for some sort of fabric lining coated and/or bonded with a metalized or "aluminized" material that will reflect back the radiant heat that would otherwise be lost through your clothing.

■ **To protect against evaporation heat loss,** wear some sort of "under" garment made of an absorbent or wicking material and be sure that the outer shell garment of your garment **system** is made with some sort of "breathable" substance that will allow excess perspiration water vapor and excess heat out of the system and not allow it to accumulate inside the garment to cause chilling and sap your heat.

**INSULATION AND WARMTH RETENTION**

# INSULATION AND WARMTH RETENTION

## RADIATION:

Radiation is the direct flow of heat from a warm source (the skin) to a cold source (the air). Body heat is directly radiated from the skin, passing through most linings, "insulating" materials and shell fabrics. However, this type of heat loss can be prevented by coating the inside of an insulating material with a micro-thin, vapor-deposited layer of aluminum or using an aluminum metalized film as a fused or bonded lining, positioned between a lining and an outer shell fabric. Unfortunately, with bonded films, in cold weather it can become stiff, "noisy" and "crinkly" when the wearer moves. Also, the vapor deposition of aluminum on the interior fibers of a fabric work fine, but its effectiveness can be reduced or lost if cleaning materials, wear and/or perspiration dulls or erodes the deposited metal. Fortunately, radiation is the least way the body heat is lost.

## CONVECTION:

Convection works on the principle that warm air is lighter than cold air and, therefore, rises. As the skin produces heat, it tends to rise and escape through the upper parts of the body (head, neck and shoulders) or through any openings or gaps in the clothing (sleeves, plackets, waists, etc.). Clothing design is the most common approach to prevent convection heat loss by creating closely fitting closures and accessories for all the spots where heat could be lost.

Therefore, accessories such as gloves, hats, caps, hoods, ear muffs and other head coverings are proper approaches to containing convection heat loss. Tight collars, turtle-necks, zip-up or button-up collars and close fitting rib trims at the neck, sleeve and ankle areas are advised. Adjustable, cinched waist areas in coats, tie-down hip huggers, sealed, overlapping plackets, close fitting, zippered pant cuffs and closely fitted boot tops and tight wrist closures on gloves are all intended to prevent both the penetration of cold air into the clothing and, more importantly, to prevent the body's warm, convection-driven "atmosphere" from escaping.

## CONDUCTION:

Conduction heat loss is most commonly addressed in fabric design, in fiberfill design and in the approach of garment layering. As the body produces heat, it warms every material it comes in contact with. This, in turn, heats that material, or, if there is only one layer of clothing, it escapes into the colder air. (It is to be noted that certain synthetic fibers have a lower heat conduction rate, or "thermal conductivity", than others. Polypropylene or olefin fibers have the lowest thermal conduction rate of all fibers and their use could contribute somewhat to the control of heat loss in fabrics containing them.)

In most cases, to stop the loss of conducted heat, three major approaches are (1) to create as many air spaces as possible in a layering

material, letting the body heat the trapped air spaces in and around the fibers, the fabrics or the layers of fabrics that are placed between the body and the outside air (down, brushed fabrics, fiberfills, etc.); (2) to create a barrier of some sort to prevent cold air (still or moving) from penetrating the insulating fabric or fabric system and sapping the trapped heat (windproofing, vapor barriers, etc.); or (3) to coat a fabric with material that will absorb, control and radiate back the body's own heat without allowing the heat to escape by conduction or radiation (Phase Change Materials).

Originally, the most common approach was just piling on layer upon layer of fabrics usually created from some sort of hair fiber with a natural "crimp" or bulk, like wool. Not only did it itch, but the layers were heavy and bulky.

Another traditional method was the use of goose or eiderdown (the very fine, insulation feathers the goose or duck grows next to his skin). It still is the classic way to insulate anything from bedding to outerwear. These feathers are very fine and fluffy and trap a lot of air, keeping the owner of a "down"- filled jacket or vest very warm, indeed. Today, down is still one of the warmest insulators available, but, like all things, there are problems with real feather down. It is expensive, it tends to "clump" up in some applications, it is very slow to dry if it gets wet. Also, although it is relatively light in weight, it can be quite bulky to wear and awkward to pack.

## EVAPORATION:

The last way body heat is lost is through the body's own system of cooling itself - evaporation. When moisture evaporates, the process draws heat from the surface from which the evaporation is taking place, cooling it. In warm conditions, this type of cooling effect is welcome and necessary for comfort. (Except when evaporation happens too quickly, as when too much moisture is presented to the air too quickly with the result of a chilling effect or that "clammy" feeling we sometimes experience when resting after heavy exercise.) Generally, warm air is "light" and very receptive to picking up moisture, except when the air becomes saturated (100% humidity) and cannot accept any more moisture. Cold air is "heavy" and not receptive to picking up moisture. The colder it gets, the less and less moisture it will accept. However, in cool and cold conditions, as the speed of evaporation slows when the air around the body cools and gets heavier and less able to hold moisture, direct evaporation of free (liquid) moisture is to be avoided in favor of the transmission of water vapor to the outside air through WPB (waterproof/breathable) fabric systems. This process greatly assists in preventing unwanted moisture condensation to build up inside the garment system in winter and can result in cooing and chilling the body.

INSULATION AND WARMTH RETENTION

# INSULATION/WARMTH RETENTION-
# A FIBERFILL SYSTEM

The object of insulating materials is to either collect and hold (or reflect) the body's heat and prevent its loss. Although there are several approaches to this problem, the method used here is to create as many "dead air" spaces as possible through the use of an insulating layer of specially designed fibers, called fiberfill, intended to trap the maximum amount of body heat without weight or bulk.

The outer layer of fabric **(a)** is a tightly woven fabric, usually a synthetic fiber taffeta or satin woven, that is tough and tear resistant, reasonably water repellent, in this case, treated with a **DWR** (**D**urable **W**ater **R**epellent finish) and is wind resistant.

The fiberfill layer **(b)** is a non-woven "pad" or "blanket" structure made from entangled fibers that create all sorts of "dead air" spaces to trap body heat among the fibers **(c)**. In addition, the fibers used to make up the "blanket' have a hollow center built-in **(d)** that traps additional air, adding to the warmth retention of the system and reducing the amount of fiber needed to maintain maximum warmth (weight and bulk reduction).

The inner layer **(e)** is designed to contain the fiberfill, but it can be constructed of an absorbent natural fiber or "wickable" synthetic fiber structure (knit or woven) to add another element of comfort to the overall system.

Moisture management is the process of moving excess moisture (perspiration) from the skin and transferring it away from the body in some manner or other for ultimate evaporation.

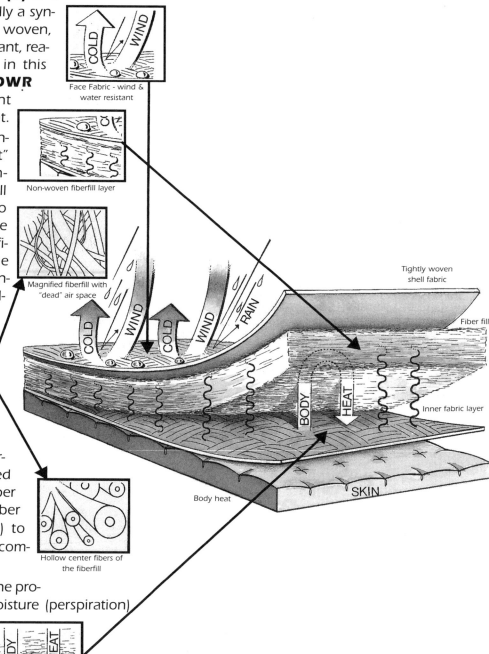

Face Fabric - wind & water resistant

Non-woven fiberfill layer

Magnified fiberfill with "dead" air space

Hollow center fibers of the fiberfill

Smooth inner fabric layer

Tightly woven shell fabric

Fiber fill

Inner fabric layer

Body heat

SKIN

# INSULATION AND WARMTH RETENTION

In this Dictionary, you will find various product approaches to insulation or heat retention, but, in general, they can be grouped into six basic approaches:

**Thermal fabrics, Fiberfills, Face Finished Fabrics, Sliver Knits, Wind Resistant Fabrics, and Phase Change Materials (PCMs)**

Let's take a quick look at each of these technical approaches to insulation and/or warmth retention:

## THERMAL FABRICS

There is a whole category of fabrics, both woven and knitted in construction, that are specifically designed to act as warm air collecting barriers to trap body heat. We are all familiar with them in their most common applications of thermal underwear or thermal blankets. They are easily recognized by the "waffle" knit or woven structure that makes them "spongy" and soft. The irregular surface of the fabric, the pattern of depressions all over the fabric and the generally loose construction are all designed to create the greatest possible number of air spaces for the body to heat. These constructions used to be made solely of cotton or wool fibers, but, today, most thermal fabrics are made of polyester, acrylics and polypropylene and have some sort of moisture management features built in as well as blends of natural and synthetic fibers. Synthetics are generally lighter in weight, shrink resistant, faster drying and less prone to any bacterial or fungal growth if put away or packed while still damp and may even be treated with anti-microbial processes.

## FIBERFILLS

Early approaches to fiberfill included everything from cotton and/or wool batting to kapok and milkweed seed hairs being stuffed between two layers of fabric to create some sort of insulation to a garment. Not being as resilient as down, with use, these fibers tended to crush and bunch together and lost most of the insulating air spaces within them. Also, they were much heavier than down and nowhere near as efficient in insulating the wearer and were easily saturated with moisture and were slow to dry.

Modern fiberfill was developed with the advent of continuous filament synthetic fibers. The first approach was to chop up the "seconds" or imperfect fibers and stuff them between two fabrics and handle the fiber the same way "down" was applied. The original fiberfill was a reasonable insulator, but tended to clump and pack together, losing much of its insulating qualities. Also, a lot of fiber had to be used to achieve good insulating properties. Later, crimping or texturing the fibers to fluff them up to trap more air made these fibers more efficient.

A much more successful approach was to form multiple ends of con-

# INSULATION/WARMTH RETENTION-
# DOUBLE SIDED KNITTED FLEECE

The object of insulating materials is to collect and hold (or reflect) as much of the body's heat production as possible.

The method illustrated here is to **(a)** create a deep, double face pile fabric structure that will provide as many trapped air spaces among the napped fibers as possible to hold body heat and keep it from escaping.

A single knitted fabric is designed and constructed to place extra high filament yarns (yarns made up of many very fine yarn strands or filaments) on both sides of the fabric structure that are designed to be brushed, napped and sheared off, like a crew cut. This creates a double faced pile fabric that is held together by **(b)** a center knitted structure that holds both front and back yarn systems in place.

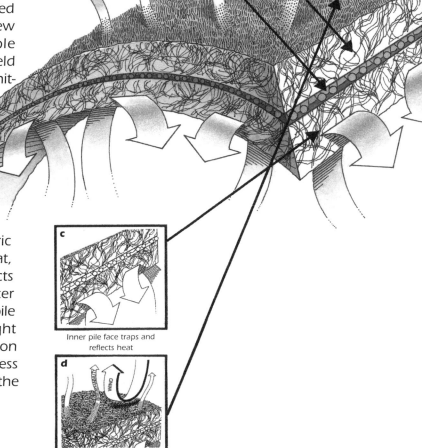

Double faced knitted pile fabric

The anchoring center knit structure

Brushed pile fibers

Knitted fabric structure

Brushed pile fibers

BREATHABILITY

WIND

The inner layer of the fabric **(c)** picks up the body heat, traps it, holds it and reflects back the excess. The outer layer **(d)** presents a dense pile face to the wind and light rain, resisting the penetration of both, while allowing excess water vapor generated by the body to escape.

Inner pile face traps and reflects heat

Outer pile repels wind but "breathes"

tinuous filament fiber into a "batting", or a blanket of fiber that was then sewn into the garment between two layers of fabric and used as a lining. It stayed in place and did not "clump" as easily. (See Illustration page 46). Another advance was to make the fibers with a hollow space(s) in the center (later, various numbers and shapes of holes). This created a dead air space in the center of each fiber strand that is warmed along with the air trapped among the fiber bundles of the fiberfill itself, thus multiplying the insulation factor of the fibers and filling material. (Some manufacturers use resins to bond the new microfibers together to create crush-resistant, down-like fiber groups, like feathers.)

Today, there is a wonderful range and selection of remarkable fiberfill products that are tremendously efficient in heat retention without bulk or weight, as well as being vermin-proof, clump-proof, fast drying, compact and, in some cases, even anti-microbial and anti-fungal.

## FACE FINISHED FABRICS

Another approach to trapping conducted body heat is with the use of face finished fabrics that are either brushed, napped or "raised" in some fashion. Fabrics range from those that have brushed or raised surfaces on one side of the fabric to those that have both sides of the fabric raised. In all cases, the raised fabric constructions create dead air spaces in and among the fibers in the "nap" or pile that traps heat and insulates the body.

It is to be noted that nearly any fabric can be "face finished" to one degree or the other, knitted or woven. However, knitted fabrics are the most commonly brushed fabrics. This is because it is easier to lay-in a separate system of yarns that is specifically designed to be brushed or napped without disturbing the yarn systems that tie the fabric together and give the fabric its strength. (This is much more difficult to do in woven fabrics.) Circular knit brushed or napped fabrics include "sweatshirt" fabrics, sliver knitted plush fabrics and many double-faced fabrics. Brushed warp knits are commonly used to create robewear fabrics, some double-sided fleeces, flannel-type fabrics and brushed linings.

## Some of the most common "face finishing" methods are:

### ▪ Sueding or "Peach Skin" Finishing

Sueding means actually sandpapering the fabric surface with sandpaper, cutting some of the surface fibers to cause the lightly "fuzzy" face characteristic of sueded fabrics. These fabrics can appear slightly 'mottled' due to special dyeing and finishing processes after sanding.

# INSULATION AND WARMTH RETENTION

When the fabric appears more smooth and uniform in appearance. it is called 'chamois-faced' or 'peach skin' finishing. Many microfiber fabrics are finished this way for the use in linings and comfort face fabrics. Insulation properties of such fabrics are minimal, but superior to unsueded fabrics.

## ▪ Brushing or Napping

This is a much more aggressive method to create a raised fabric face. A special napping or brushing machine is equipped with specialized raising or cutting wires that rapidly rotate on special cylinders while pressing into the fabric face fibers. These steel wires are designed to tug and pull at the fibers, either breaking them or just pulling them up onto small loops or "plushes" or "fleece". Sometimes the intent is to break the fibers to create a surface that will later be combed, straightened and sheared (cut evenly by a blade) to form a "velour" or "velvet" vertical pile face. Such fabrics have good warmth retention, depending upon the depth of the "pile" or "plush". The deeper the pile, the more warm air is trapped and the warmer the fabric.

If the fabric is designed with enough fiber on both sides of the fabric, the fabric can be brushed on both sides, creating the double-sided plushes and fleeces. (See Illustration page 48). The synthetic fiber versions of this type of fabric are very popular today in the performance apparel business and rightly so. They offer excellent warmth without weight, are easy care and, with new knitting and printing techniques, they now offer a wonderful variety of color, design and texture.

## SLIVER KNITS

There is a knitting system that allows the knitter to knit-in extra fiber in the back of the usual knitted structure to create a surface that can be brushed into a plush or deep pile fabric face. The extra fiber bundles are loose, but parallel, staple (pre-cut lengths of fiber or the natural fiber length) fibers, called "sliver". This is actually a stage of fiber preparation in ring spinning before the final yarn is drawn, twisted and finished. Generally, the "sliver knit" fabric face is brushed or combed to remove loose fibers and then is sheared or cut to a desired pile height. What results is a deep, plush pile fabric that is quite soft and traps a lot of body heat. These constructions can be double-faced and are quite wind resistant, as well. Some are even treated with a moisture management finish that helps wick away excess perspiration for added comfort.

## WINDPROOFING

Every fabric is made up of a system of fibers and yarns arranged in a particular way to create a fabric structure. In the process, a whole bunch of tiny gaps are created in the fabric structure. When an untreated

# INSULATION AND WARMTH RETENTION

or unprotected fabric is exposed to moving air, it allows wind-driven air to penetrate the fabric, potentially sapping the body's heat reserve.

Windproofing a fabric is not complicated. The tiny holes in the fabric structure must be filled up or filled in to block the wind. Some of the early answers were to coat the fabric with some sort of impenetrable material, such as wax, varnish or oil or, perhaps, a resin, a foam material or a film of some kind. These approaches keep the wind and perhaps the rain out of the fabric, but they would also seal in any escaping water vapor and heat the body would produce. The water vapor could condense inside the fabric or garment structure, making the wearer moist and uncomfortable.

Today, most windproofing approaches involve special coatings or membranes that have extremely tiny holes built into them, so small that they block any passage of wind or moisture into the garment while allowing the water vapor and heat to escape easily. These are called **WPB** or **W**ater**p**roof/**B**reathable systems and are described in depth later in the book.

The latest approach is to create very finely woven fabric structures made from synthetic microfibers that are very supple, yet so tightly made that nearly all the gaps remaining in the fabric structure are far smaller than water droplets and are nearly impervious to air penetration, but

will allow limited water vapor escape for breathability. All this is accomplished without coatings or backing materials of any sort.

## PHASE CHANGE MATERIALS

This is a totally different approach to warmth retention that has literally grown out of "Space Age" research. Instead of relying upon heated air spaces, as in traditional feather, fiberfill and brushed or napped materials, this technology creates its temperature regulating effect by applying a thin coating of millions of tiny microscopic beads (microPCMs), each containing a special "phase changing material" that gradually changes from a solid to a liquid within the bead as it absorbs body heat. This heat retention is spread uniformly throughout the coated material and radiates the heat back to the body to keep it comfortably warm. The same physical principle by which it stays comfortably warm also prevents it from overheating, thus giving protection even in warmer environments. Because it is not dependent upon gaps and air spaces, like the traditional "insulators", its effectiveness is not affected by squeezing or compression (which reduces air spaces that hold warmth) or moisture content (when "fills" get wet, the water takes up the air spaces and insulation is reduced). These unique microPCM beads can be built into synthetic fibers when they are made, or, more commonly, are used as a coating for almost any type of material or substrate.

51

# INSULATION

## ACTIVIST®

When you need a body-hugging, fleece fabric that resists snagging and sheds snow, you might want to try **Patagonia's Activist®** polyester/nylon and Lycra® spandex fleece. Whether for full length, two-way stretch bibs, tops or tights, this fabric is designed for cold weather alpine climbing, skiing, cold weather track training, trail running, cross country skiing, etc. In addition, Activist® fleece is treated with a special anti-microbial finish that won't let microbes, fungus or yeast develop on the fabric, preventing odors and unsightly staining and discoloration of the fabric.

## adidas EQT TRI-QUILT™

If lightweight insulation is what you're looking for, consider **adidas America's EQT Tri-Quilt™** fabric. It is made with two layers of soft polyester double knit fabrics quilted together with a light fiberfill in the middle. The top and bottom fabrics are knitted to give the system great "give & go" flexibility. The inside fabric layer is made of microfiber for extra softness next to the skin, while the fiberfill in the middle is lightweight, air-textured polyester fibers that offer good insulation for all but the most extreme conditions. The fabrics have been treated with a wicking agent that allows the fabrics to easily transport moisture to keep the athlete comfortable. Originally designed for soccer "goalies", Tri-Quilt™ is now finding a home in tops and pants for all sorts of performance challenges.

## ARCTIC FLEECE®

**Menra Mills** offers a 100% polyester, double-faced fleece fabric that is warm and soft, offering excellent warmth without weight, quick drying and wind resistance. With easy care performance, this fabric is ideal for tops, outdoor wear, and other mid-layer or outer layer apparel for tough conditions.

## BERBER by GLENOIT®

One cannot live by plushes and piles alone! **Glenoit Mills** steps forward with a softly curled fabric face made with sliver knit pile technology that offers not only a great 'boiled wool', poodle-like look but also a luxurious fabric with great warmth retention without weight and with breathable comfort. Once again, both the appearance and performance of the fabric rests firmly on the special blend of fibers combined in the sliver yarns, only this time a 'hair' fiber is sparsely introduced for texture and color contrast in dyeing (a subtle heather and 'flecked' coloring is present). When the hair yarn and heather effect is not used, Glenoit calls the fabric Zendura®.

## CHINELLA®

When it comes to heavier weight double-faced fleece, **Menra's Chinella®** fabric must be up there with the best. With a velour-like sheared face, the fabric is made of 100% low pill polyester that has been specially treated to transport moisture (wick) away from the body for dry comfort. Easy care and quick drying, the fabric will keep you warm and

cozy in either shell applications or mid-layer garments in extreme conditions, as in skiwear and performance outerwear.

## CHINELLA LITE®

The lightweight champ at **Menra Mills**, **Chinella Lite®** has all the virtues and performance of its heavier weight sister fabric, but is lighter and perfect for the transitional season outerwear needs for golf, running, cycling and hiking. Also, it is the ideal weight to wear under a performance shell garment to add moisture management and insulation to the "system" for extreme conditions.

## CITIFLEECE™

This double-brushed sportswear and warm-up fleece from **Dyersburg** features a sheared, luxurious velour face that is designed to keep the wearer warm and cozy. Made of Fortrel® Spunnaire™, low pill polyester, **Citifleece™** is treated with a 3M Scotchgard® finish that adds durable soil and stain release as well as an enhanced wicking for moisture management.

## CLOUD 9 FLEECE™

Here is **Pearl Izumi's** double-faced fleece fabric for activewear and athleisure apparel. It is a knitted construction made from low-pill, microdenier polyester for soft, luxurious comfort and long-term good looking wear. It is designed to have excellent, lofted coverage, providing high heat insulation value and breathability while offering

stretchable comfort and fit and wind protection.

## DENSIFIED BATTING

When the name of the game is fiberfill and trapping heat, the size of the individual fibers and the number of fibers per square inch in the fiberfill are both key indicators of insulation efficiency. **Bonded Fibers and Quilting** have devised a proprietary method that "densifies" a 3 denier per filament polyester fiber batting and packs in a maximum amount of fiber into the smallest space. Called **Densified Batting**, it is claimed to increase the heat retention of the fiberfill and, at the same time, reduces the overall bulk of the batting in the linings and quilting.

## DYERSBURG E.C.O.®

**E.C.O.®** is **Dyersburg Corporation's** brand for a high performance, plush fleece fabric made from 87% Fortrel® EcoSpun® recycled polyester staple fiber. Reputed to have low-pill performance (undoubtedly helped not only by the fiber, but also from the clean, sheared surface), E.C.O. fleece makes a warm, wind and water resistant shell fabric for outerwear, tops, sportswear and accessories. Bet you never knew that old soft drink bottles could be so comfortable!

## DYERSBURG E.C.O.® LITE

This is a lighter weight version of **Dyersburg Corporation's E.C.O.®** fleece fabric, containing 85% of fine denier-per-filament, re-cycled

# INSULATION

Wellman Fortrel® EcoSpun® polyester. It is a knitted, double-sided fleece fabric that is not weight restricted to any particular season for outerwear, sportswear and accessories year round.

## DYERSBURG E.C.O. WOOL®

As the name implies, **E.C.O. Wool®** is **Dyersburg's** blend of Wellman's EcoSpun® re-cycled polyester staple fiber and of Wellman's patented washable wool fiber in an itch-proof, low-pill velour fabric that provides superior warmth without weight. (Wool is sometimes described as the "perfect fiber" because it has a natural crimp that makes it an excellent insulator and makes it 'springy' and resilient. It also has a "medulla" or spongy center inside the fiber to absorb and transfer moisture and a tough outer surface for evaporation.) In addition, because both wool and polyester do not burn very well, the fabrics are flame resistant and are machine washable without fear of shrinkage. Naturally, a user friendly and ecologically friendly blend, look for E.C.O. Wool® in outerwear, sportswear and other active apparel.

## ECOPILE®

**Draper Knitting Co.** offers a collection of insulating shell and/or lining fabrics made from napped 100% recycled EcoSpun® polyester fibers from Wellman Fibers produced with a variety of backings and meshes for selected performance apparel applications. Available are a broad selection of fabrics including a breathable film and eyelet mesh laminated to a brushed shell for increased breathability, a double-sided finish **(EcoPile® II)** for increased insulation and a bonded brushed tricot back (reduces overall weight) to satisfy various performance needs.

## ECOTHERM®

The patented, down-like cousin of **Albany International's** Primaloft® fiberfill product, **Ecotherm®** is made of at least 50% re-cycled polymer-based products and is ecologically friendly. Even so, EcoTherm® offers the consumer the same superior down-like insulation performance, as well as water and wind resistant performance, as Albany's other fiberfill product. Performance outerwear and accessories, athleisure and footwear now feature nature-friendly EcoTherm® insulation.

## GLENAURA®

**Glenoit Mills** has utilized sliver-knit pile technology (the knitting technique of knitting in and locking in untwisted fiber bundles on the face of a fabric to create a plush or pile fabric) combined with special, proprietary spun synthetic yarn blends as the pile fibers to create a very soft, sheared, velvety pile fabric. Aside from the knitted-in patterning and sculptured patterns, the **Glenaura®** collection offers wonderful insulation and warmth retention. The fabric's breathable, water and wind resistance, as well as moisture management, grow

# INSULATION

out of the unique performance character of the company's proprietary spun blends of acrylic and polyester fibers. These are most commonly used as an outer shell layer or lining of outdoor sportswear and outerwear.

## GLENPILE®

**Glenoit** uses fine gauge sliver knitting technology with special blends of polyester, acrylic, micro-fine acrylic and other performance fibers in tightly secured, but not twisted yarn bundles to create the **Glenpile®** fabric's face. The individual fibers in these fiber bundles "bloom out" in finishing, allowing them to do their performance magic without interference from the other fibers used to tie the fabric construction together. Result? Each fiber in the pile of the fabric does its special "thing", such as wicking away moisture, or providing special insulation, or water resistance, breathability, etc. Plus the fabric is soft and cuddly for all those outer layer or lining applications in sportswear or outerwear.

## HIGHLANDER™

**Coville's** trademark for a family of surface interest, "Sherpa" loop textured circular knitted poly/cotton fabrics that feature low shrinkage, a soft, comfortable hand and a wonderful fine textured and lightly brushed face. The companion fabric group is called **Highlander Plus™**and features a special top-dyed polyester fiber spun into the face yarns of the circular knit. This produces a heather effect to the "Sherpa"- textured fabric face as well

as a full range of variegated textures and patterns. Both of these fabric collections are used in tops and bottoms for everything from surfer beachwear to cold weather pullovers and warmups.

## HOLLOFIL II®

**Hollofil®** fibers are just what **DuPont** says they are. With four hollow chambers built into the center of the fiber itself to trap the body's warm air before it escapes, this fiberfill design is 20% more efficient in insulation than solid-fiber insulating fiberfills. Available in two grades, the **Hollofil II®** fibers are moisture resistant, easy care and affordable. Look for it in kids outerwear, value priced outerwear and general outdoor wear.

## KINDERFLEECE®

One of the driving needs for the creation of active, performance wear probably originated to keep children from wearing holes in themselves at play and then were adapted by adults after they saw how much fun the kids were having. **Dyersburg Corporation** has adapted its double-sided fleece using Wellman's Fortrel® Spunnaire® polyester fibers and engineered a fabric especially designed for kids. Light, soft and cuddly, **Kinderfleece®** is more than a pretty face - it is tough enough for the most active child and yet is easy care and super soil release, thanks to the 3M Scotchgard® Stain Release® process that is used with every yard. In addition, the same process helps a lot with

55

# INSULATION

moisture management and the fabrics have good flame resistant performance and safety built in.

## LIFA® ARCTIC

**Lifa® Arctic** from **Helly-Hansen** focuses on insulation as its primary function with controlled moisture management as the secondary consideration. The special knitted fabric system is constructed using a 100% spun and napped polypropylene "thermal" layer next to the skin ( for insulation and moisture transfer), covered with a special spun blend of polypropylene and wool ("Prowool") on the outside of the fabric. Both layers trap a lot of air for insulation and the Prowool layer pulls the body moisture from the inner wicking (and insulating) layer to the outside of the fabric for controlled evaporation. The interior fabric layer keeps the blended wool fibers in the outer layer away from the skin where they could cause allergenic or itching problems. All this makes for very comfortable and functional body fitting underwear.

## MICROART®

**Unitika America** is offering a technically advanced, fine denier nylon yarn for shell fabrics. The yarn has a multi-axial hollow cross section that traps air warmed by the body both within the fiber itself as well as between the fibers that make up the lightweight, brushed and bulked fabrics produced with them. In addition, these **Microart®** fibers are supposed to have very good water resistance to keep the wearer dry. All sorts of outdoor clothes, skiwear and snowboarding gear are among the product mix for Microart®.

## MICRO-LOFT®

Today's microfiber technology is brought to fiberfill by **DuPont** with very warm results, without weight or bulk. DuPont's **Micro-loft®** fiberfill is finer than silk, soft as down, non-allergenic, moisture resistant and warmer per-inch than down. Not only that, it retains its insulating values when damp and it dries quickly. It is available in two loft qualities, but the big news is the way it compacts into a small space and springs back with soft drapability. High performance skiwear and outerwear jackets, vests and bibs are just a few of the warm wear applications you will discover using Micro-loft®.

## MICRO-PLUSH™

For lightweight warmth and breathability, **Monterey Mills** offers a microdenier acrylic plush fabric that serves well in both warm and cold climates. The natural polarity of acrylic (electrical positive and negative charges at each end of the fiber molecule) is said to interact with water molecules (which are "bi-polar" too). This means much of the perspiration easily moves through the fabric in water vapor form to evaporate and dissipate in the air, keeping the fabric unsaturated and the wearer comfortable. The fabric stays antistatic as well. Warm outerwear and sportswear are the applications here.

# INSULATION

## N/SL8™

**Monterey Mills** has created a special two-faced, beefy, sliver knit fabric that is made of 100% re-cycled, polyester that they call **N/SL8**™("In-Sul-8" - get it?). The face side has a deep sliver knit pile for excellent insulation properties and softness as well as water resistance while, on the inside, there is a napped face for warm, cozy comfort next to the skin. Moisture management is built in with a natural "push-pull" movement between the thirsty napped inside layer picking up the moisture while the dense, face fibers of the plush pick up the water and move it out through the pile fibers to the surface for evaporation. The result is a warm, hard wearing, comfortable, water resistant fabric ideal for outerwear and sportswear.

## NEOPRENE®

**DuPont Dow Elastomers L.L.C.** are the source for this historic performance product for activewear. Whether you surf or dive in all weather conditions, **Neoprene®'s** special "closed cell" artificial foam rubber keeps you warm, dry and insulated from those sharp things in the water. Because of its excellent insulating qualities, its non-absorbency and its extraordinary durability, garments made from sheets of cellular Neoprene® foam are the cold water and weather choice in or on the water. These "wet suits" have all the seams joined using Neoprene®-based adhesives to keep them watertight.

Also, look for Neoprene® foam products in the sponge soles of a wide range of shoes and boots.

## NORDIC SPIRIT®

**Huntingdon Mills** presents their collection of sliver knit pile fabrics for outerwear that are designed to keep you warm in cold weather. Sliver knit is made by having untwisted, but parallel, fiber bundles, called "sliver", specially knitted and locked into a knitted base fabric. The result is a very plush fabric face that is then fully "bloomed" (relaxed) and sheared to even out the fabric face. **Nordic Spirit®** has acrylic and/or polyester fibers making up the plush face and tough polyester fibers holding the fabric structure together. Acrylic is designed to be a good moisture transfer vehicle as are the polyester base fibers; therefore, this fabric is reputed to be a good moisture manager. Also, the density of the pile keeps the wind out very effectively.

## OUTLAST™

This product brings a new technological approach to the problem of insulation, heat retention and over-heating . **Outlast Technologies** is bringing the space age concept of "Phase Change Materials" (PCM) to the arena of performance apparel insulation. Instead of relying on heated air spaces, as in traditional fiberfill insulating materials, the **Outlast**™technology creates its warming effect by applying a thin coating of millions of microscopic beads (microPCM's), each containing a special "phase change" material that gradually changes from a solid to a liquid within the bead as it absorbs body heat. This heat retention is spread uniformly throughout the coated material and radiates the heat back to the body to keep it comfortably warm. (This same principle also prevents it from becoming overheated, even in a warmer environment.) Because the micro PCM coating is not dependent upon gaps and air spaces as in a traditional insulating fabric or fill, its effectiveness is not affected by compression (squeezing or crushing, reducing the air spaces to hold warmth) or moisture content (the more moisture in the fiberfill, the less room for trapped air spaces). This process can be applied in synthetic fiber manufacturing or it may be coated on practically any fabric substrate or may also be used in conjunction with other insulation systems to enhance and broaden their performance range.

## POLARGUARD® 3D

The newest of the Polarguard "family" of continuous filament fiberfills, **Trevira's Polarguard® 3D** features the high-void cross section (hollow center) that traps warm air, prevents the collapse of the fiber, which could cause "bunching" and uneven distribution, and adds warmth without weight. The special features of the 3D version of Polarguard® is that it is finer and softer than its "sister" products and the warmth vs. weight ratios are the highest yet offered without sacrificing the durability, loft retention,

extended life insulation and wet insulating abilities. Whether in jackets, vests, or sleeping bags, Polarguard® 3D is one of the warmest out there.

## POLARGUARD® HV

**Polarguard® HV** (**H**igh **V**oid continuous filament) is **Trevira's** improvement on its long standing Polarguard® fiberfill product for insulation. This "hybrid" fiber has a large hollow center cavity inside the fiber that traps air warmed by the body and reduces the weight of overall fiber for its size. This results in a superior warmth-to-weight ratio that is on a par with down. Used in a wide range of insulated apparel, Polarguard® HV is highly compressible, resists wet conditions, dries quickly and, because it is a continuous filament insulation, it does not pull apart, clump or mat as other staple-form fiberfills do.

## POLARTEC®

**Polartec®** is the umbrella trademark used by **Malden Mills** to identify their broad range of brushed, treated and laminated performance insulating fabrics intended for a wide range of performance apparel from underwear to extreme "element control" applications. In order to assure consistent quality in the products carrying their Polartec® trademarks and tags, the use of the marks is subject to the conditions of a licensing arrangement between Malden and its apparel or accessory manufacturing customer.

# INSULATION

## POLARTEC® 100 SERIES

**Malden Mills** offers its strong **Polartec®** family of double-brushed (napped) performance fabrics that could claim to be the fabric program that "re-legitimized" polyester as a premium performance fiber in the textile market. As part of that revolution, the **Polartec® 100** Series is a collection of lightweight thermal fabrics that are designed to be the first layer of any clothing system. With excellent warmth retention and anti-microbial (anti-bacteria and fungus resistant) performance, these fabrics readily wick moisture away from the body and allow the moisture vapor escape for breathable comfort while keeping you warm. Perfect for underwear, shirts and other lighter weight performance apparel.

## POLARTEC® 200 SERIES

The **Polartec® 200 Series** is the "work-horse" intermediate weight of the **Malden Polartec®** family of insulating fabrics. Used either for an outer garment application, like jackets, pullovers, pants, vests or shorts, or as an intermediate layer garment, the double-faced napped fabric offers excellent warmth retention without weight, good water repellency, breathability and a wide range of textured and 'shearling' textures. Made primarily of environmentally friendly recycled polyester fibers, the fabrics are treated to be anti-microbial and mildew proof.

## POLARTEC® 300 SERIES

The **Polartec®** "heavyweight" champ of warmth (but, of course, without the weight!), the **Polartec® 300 Series** is the top of the line in **Malden's** warm-wear fabric collection with excellent warmth retention and insulation, good water repellence and breathable comfort built in. The fabric is said to be non-pilling, is treated to resist bacteria and mildew formation and is made primarily from recycled polyester polymer. Definitely a serious outerwear fabric designed for jackets, vests, pants and other performance cold weather wear.

## POLARTEC® POWERSTRETCH

This fabric group from **Malden** is designed to be worn next to the skin to offer maximum moisture management and breathable comfort to the working athlete. Especially constructed with fine fibers on both faces of this double-sided fabric, the inner surface next to the skin draws the moisture away from the skin, moving it to the outer layer that spreads it out for rapid evaporation. In addition, the construction of the fabric allows the body's water vapor to escape easily, keeping the subject dry and comfortable even during heavy exercise. With Malden's anti-microbial protection built in, this collection of lighter weight performance fabrics is ideal for shirting, tops, underwear and sportswear.

# INSULATION

## POLARTEC® 200 SERIES BI-POLAR

This intermediate weight, double-sided performance insulating fabric from **Malden** offers two very different faces. The outer surface of the fabric is tightly constructed to achieve maximum abrasion and wear resistance while the lofty "shearling"-length inner surface provides excellent thermal insulation (and it's breathable, of course). Ideally suited to performance apparel used as an intermediate layer or as an outer garment, such as jackets, pants, vests, shorts and pullovers.

## POLARTEC® 300 SERIES BI-POLAR

The "Boss" performer in the class, the **Polartec® 300 Series Bi-Polar** fabric group is 'expedition weight' with high-tech, high-performance protection built in. **Malden** designed this group of fabrics to be the top performers in durability, high performance efficiency and attractiveness. Offering the famous double faces of the Polartec® family, this group has a highly durable, wind and water resistant, low brushed face with a comfortable, breathable and superior moisture management, "shearling" inner surface that gives excellent insulation from body heat loss. These fabrics are light in weight, compress easily for packing and can be found in jackets, pants, pullovers, vests, shorts and all kinds of warm apparel for a cold world.

## POLARTEC® MICRO SERIES

Microfibers come to **Malden Mills**. Here is a collection of ultra-light fabrics designed to be worn next to the skin or not far away made from microfiber yarns that allow for a tight construction that improves wind and water resistance. In addition, the **Polartec® Micro Series** of fabrics are lightly sueded to give a wonderful chamois-like hand for friendly warm comfort. Add to this a low pill, wickable, moisture management finish and you have just the fabrics for performance shirting, underwear, cross-over wear and other sports apparel applications.

## POLARTEC® THERMAL STRETCH GROUP

Just when you thought that **Malden Mills** was only interested in freezing temperatures and howling winter winds, along comes a whole new generation of performance fabrics designed to address the challenges of the sea and the surf. **The Polartec® Thermal Stretch Group** of fabrics challenges neoprene as the champion in warm wetwear. The heavier version is designed for wet suit diving in tropical waters and for cycling gear. It offers excellent heat loss protection (protects against conduction and radiation heat loss with a napped fabric against the skin), superior abrasion resistance, four way stretch, thanks to a 10% Lycra® spandex content. It also offers neutral buoyancy and breathability with-

out water penetration, thanks to a special breathable membrane used to laminate together the face and back fabrics.

A lighter weight "dry suit" fabric is available and designed for above-water sports such as paddling, surfing, water skiing and sailing. With a bonded/laminated polyurethane water-shedding face attached to a polyester and Lycra® spandex, anti-microbial treated fleece, the fabric sheds water (it can also be made totally waterproof with seam sealing) and retains body heat by blocking all kinds of heat loss. Now **Polartec®** will perform for you both above and below the water line!

## PRIMALOFT®

**Primaloft®** is a patented microfiber insulating fiberfill from **Albany International** that is supposed to closely resemble goosedown in both its physical and thermal properties - but, in windy, wet conditions, this product repels both elements very efficiently, yet stays light in weight, warm and dry. In addition, it is hypo-allergenic for those allergic to feathers, compresses like down but bounces back every time and won't "clump". Found readily in all sorts of performance wear (as the fiberfill layer between the shell fabric and the liner), fashion outerwear and accessories, Primaloft® is available in two designs with different performance characteristics identified as PL-1 and PL-2.

## PROPILE®

**Helly-Hansen** offers a collection of three double-brushed pile fabrics especially designed to keep you warm and comfortable in most conditions. Knitted with a special "Fiberlock" knitting technique that locks in the pile fibers for durability and superior after-wash appearance, the fabrics are made of wickable polyester for moisture transport and breathability as well as insulation. Available in heavy, medium and lightweight pile height and density, the consumer has a choice depending upon need or function. Pullovers, jackets, pants, light climbing gear and general activewear are available in all three weights of fabric carrying the **Propile®** hangtag.

## QUALLOFIL®

Especially engineered with seven holes positioned on the inside of each fiber to trap extra warmth, **DuPont's Quallofil®** fiberfill is claimed to be 25% warmer than down when damp and is supposed to dry three times faster than down. Water resistant and breathable, it is designed to be the manmade replacement for real goosedown insulation. It is non-allergenic, easy care and machine washable, it always holds its shape and its insulating properties even after repeated cleanings. This high-loft insulation is found in all sorts of cold weather protective clothing, rugged outdoor wear and high performance skiwear.

# INSULATION

## REPLEX™

**Replex™** incorporates a very fine denier polyester fiber in a tightly woven fabric from **Toray** that has excellent wind resistance and very good water repellence, making it excellent for lightweight windbreakers and warmups in tennis, golf, biking and other light activewear uses. Treated with a durable DWR finish to assure the best protection from water penetration, Replex™ will keep you dry and comfortable in most conditions.

## REPLEX™ LIGHT

**Toray** presents a high fashion performance activewear fabric with a smooth, microfiber touch and a special surface texture that looks great! Tightly woven, like its "namesake", it, too, is treated with a durable DWR finish that shuts out rain but allows the fabric to "breathe". **Replex™ Light** is ideal for tennis, soccer, golf, aerobic sports, jogging and cycling.

## SNO-TEC®

**Dorma Mills** offers a new warp-knitted polyester fleece fabric for jacket linings, warmups, shirts and other lightweight sports and sportswear apparel. Napped on one side, the fabric is warm, lightweight, abrasion resistant and is inherently flame retardant.

## THERMA F.I.T.®

**Nike's** double-brushed microdenier fleece fabric is the thermal layer of their F.I.T. garment system. Made in a very tightly knitted fabric structure using microfibers for maximum coverage and density without bulk or weight, the fabric acts as a wind barrier as well as an excellent insulation against the loss of body heat. Because of its lower bulk, the **Therma F.I.T.®** double-sided fleece allows free movement for highly aerobic activities. The fabric is ideal either in an outer garment or as a second insulating garment layer, perhaps used for running, hiking, snowboarding, skiing, climbing, cycling or training.

## THERMA FLEECE

Imagine a fabric with a looped back, brushed fleece on the inside for insulation; knit in some spandex fibers for excellent stretch and recovery and create a smooth, hard-wearing fabric face made with either nylon or polyester for superior durability. Add to this a special wicking finish on the inside to provide exceptional moisture management and you have **Pearl Izumi's Therma Fleece** fabric that's ideal for running, cycling and other winter-active sports.

## THERMOLITE®

**Thermolite®** is **DuPont's** thin fiberfill insulation material made from 80% pre-consumer recycled polyester (not from polyester that is made into a product, sold and used by a consumer and then recycled - like soft drink bottles- to be re-used as another fiber or product). This polyester, recycled "seconds" or unusable polymer

waste product left over from other polyester fiber or product manufacturing processes, is designed to give a maximum amount of insulation with a minimum of bulk. Non-allergenic, it is claimed to be 10% warmer than comparable thin insulation materials and stays 25% warmer after several cleanings. Available in three varieties, Thermolite® is ideal for all sorts of snow sports, outerwear, biking and golf apparel and rainwear linings; it also ends up in boot and shoe linings as well.

## THERMOLOFT®

This is **DuPont's** "mid-loft" insulating fiberfill with a hollow space built into the center cross section of the fiber. It is said to offer 30% warmer cold weather protection than other branded thin insulating materials with less bulk plus added softness and superior fiber migration control (the tendency for some types of fibers to "poke through" the containing fabric layers of a quilt or lining) without the use of non-woven scrims. Made from 80% "pre-consumer" polyester (see above), **Thermoloft®** is ideal for high performance skiwear, snow mobiling, hunting gear and general cold weather performance outerwear.

## THINSULATE™

This is **3M's** "benchmark" fiberfill trademark quality control licensing program built around a family of thin, lightweight synthetic insulation materials made from synthetic microfibers claimed to be 1 ½ times to 2 times warmer than natural goosedown and other polyester insulations with equal thickness. The use of any of the several **Thinsulate™** trademarks and products is conditional on the licensing of the end use manufacturer by 3M to apply the insulating products in a manner that satisfies the strict standards of application set forth by 3M in their agreement. Thinsulate™ fiberfill products can be found in a broad range of cold weather garments.

## THINSULATE™ LITE LOFT®

Here is the **3M** answer to warmth without weight in its high performance fiberfill range of products. Made from ultra-fine thermal bonded fibers, this product is claimed to be the most weight efficient, low density synthetic insulation material on the market. Made from 77% polyester and 23% polyolefin microfibers, **Thinsulate™ Lite Loft®** insulation retains its insulating ability even in damp conditions. Look for it in skiwear, performance outerwear and sleeping bags.

## THINSULATE™ ULTRA

This is a mid-loft, thin, compressible member of 3M's **Thinsulate™** family of ultra thin, ultra warm insulating products. It is made of 55% polyester and 45% polyolefin for maximum water resistance and breathable protection. This keeps you warm and comfortable in damp conditions without weight, yet with maximum softness and minimum bulk. General outer-

# INSULATION

wear, sportswear and accessories are the most common applications for **Thinsulate™ Ultra**.

## WORSTERLON®

This rugged outerwear fabric from **Milliken & Co.** looks and feels like real woven wool melton, except it is made from 100% spun polyester and doesn't itch or cause any skin irritation! It is woven with a special construction that is napped on both sides for added heat retention and comfort. The fabric has good moisture management and soil release and the polyester content assures easy care, machine washability, quick drying, wrinkle resistance and hard wearing performance. Hunting clothes and good looking outerwear will be carrying the **Worsterlon®** tags.

## YUKON 2000®

The heavier step up from Yukon Fleece® is **Huntingdon's Yukon 2000®** double-faced velour (sheared plush). Made of low pill polyester for hard wear, this warm winner for high performance shell applications demonstrates an excellent "push-pull" moisture management plus excellent warmth retention and wind resistance. This one you can wear outside in the cold, unless there is a brisk wind blowing - then you might want a totally windproof shell over that Yukon 2000® velour top to totally cut the wind. The velour takes care of the rest of your insulation needs.

## YUKON FLEECE®

When it comes to cold, Canada is right down there with some of the lowest of the low temperatures in the book - and, if anyone knows, the Canadians know how to stay warm. **Yukon Fleece®** is the product of **Huntingdon Mills** in Quebec, Canada and it is designed to keep you warm without weight. A circular knit fleece made of tough polyester, napped and sheared on one or both sides (usually sold as a two-sided fleece), Yukon Fleece® offers insulation as well as the natural wicking action of the hydrophobic polyester fibers for moisture management. It is an "everyday" performance fabric for medium duty outerwear.

## YUKON PROTEC®

When the going really gets rough in the Yukon, Sgt. Preston probably reaches for his coat made from **Yukon Protec®**, **Huntingdon Mills'** laminate shell fabric. It features an inside velour face for insulation and warmth, a special laminated, impervious but breathable membrane that keeps out the wicked winds and the snow, sleet or rain. This bonded barrier fabric allows moisture vapor to escape but stops much of the cold air penetration. The special membrane bonding system allows the fabric system to stretch in all directions without fear of de-lamination or peeling. A great fabric for performance outerwear or for the suburbanite going out for provisions on a cold and miserable winter's day.

# MANAGING THE BODY'S AIR CONDITIONING AND WATER SYSTEM

# MOISTURE MANAGEMENT

## STAYING DRY AND COMFORTABLE
## WHILE STAYING ACTIVE

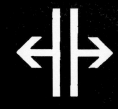

**Perspiration is the natural cooling process of the body.** The problem is dealing with excess moisture production and how to deal with it efficiently in normal conditions. It should be noted that conditions of high heat and humidity and cold conditions greatly reduce moisture evaporation in all forms (liquid or vapor).

The **key strategies** in performance active, base layer garments are:

- **Absorbency -** The ability of a hydrophilic (water loving) fiber to take water into itself, moving it through the actual structure of the fiber (and, in the case of cotton and wool, into a hollow or spongy core where it flows to the outside of the fiber) as well as over, along and around the fiber surface for evaporation. This is a property of natural fibers and some synthetics, such as acetate, rayon and, to a degree, nylon.

- **Adsorbancy -** The property of some water hating (hydrophobic) synthetic fibers to encourage water to flow along, around and over (but not through) the fibers to be carried away for evaporation. This process is generally called "wicking". If this property is not built (inherent) into the fiber, some fibers can be chemically treated to enhance their "wicking" properties.

- **Ionization** - The chemical treatment of fabrics to create an electrical charge or polarization of a fiber or fabric that prevents much of the moisture from staying in liquid form. It remains in vapor state, escaping the fabric for dissipation.

- **Push-Pull Moisture Management** - A fabric system that is created with the skin side of the fabric made from a hydrophobic (water hating) fiber that is treated to wick moisture. This lets it pick up the moisture and transfer it to adjoining fabric layer that is made of an absorbent hydrophilic (water loving) fibers that transfer the moisture it to the fabric face where it spreads out for evaporation. This same "capillary" action can be achieved by the use of two layers of the same fiber type but with two different degrees of fiber fineness (denier per filament) in each layer with very good results.

- **Activities** where moisture management is important include running, aerobics, in-line skating, cross-country, skiing, swimming, team sports, etc., etc.

MOISTURE MANAGEMENT

# MOISTURE MANAGEMENT

## MANAGING THE BODY'S AIR CONDITIONING AND WATER SYSTEM

From the title, it appears we are approaching the body's control mechanisms like the operational systems running a building. Not a bad analogy.

If you want to keep a building from losing heat, you insulate it in some manner. If it is buffeted by cold winds, you seal off all possible ways the cold air can penetrate the structure by plugging up all the cracks and crevices and covering the window openings with drapes, blinds or storm windows. If it is too warm inside, you either open the windows and doors, put vents and fans of some sort in the windows and in the attic to carry off the heat or you find some way to "refrigerate" or "air condition" the building. If there is too much condensation inside the house, you try to find a way to ventilate the building without allowing the rain and wind to come in. If the basement leaks, you find some type of pump to get the worst out and use absorbent materials to mop up with. And so forth...

When we develop performance fibers, fabrics and finishes to hold in the body's heat, to ventilate it and cool it down, to get rid of unwanted perspiration or water vapor or to accomplish all of the above while keeping out the elements, our control and management design approaches tend to be nearly identical to those used to manage a building's heat and water systems. Of course, the major differences are a matter of scale and the fact that the body's mechanisms and needs are changing constantly, that the whole system is in constant motion and that the occupant also wants to be comfortable, mobile and look good even in the most extreme conditions. Some job!

## THE TROUBLE WITH WATER

A good place to start is with water. The human body is primarily made up of water. Generally, we are not aware of the basic properties of that vital liquid and so it is difficult to understand how water is used by the body to regulate its heat, how it reacts to the skin, the air and the other materials surrounding or in contact with it.

Nearly everyone knows that water is made up of hydrogen and oxygen ($H_2O$). This basic water molecule is "bi-polar", having a positive charge on one end of the molecule and a negative charge at the other end. Essentially, this makes water into a magnet-like substance and, indeed, water molecules seem to act accordingly.

One of the most easily observed results of that property is in water's "beading", or characteristic tendency to clump together in spherical drops in the air or as tiny "puddles" or droplets on a surface. These rounded shapes are caused by what is called "surface tension" or the water molecule's magnetic pull to link itself together with other water molecules to form a "skin" around the liquid, greatly reducing its dissipation (spreading) and evaporation. (As a matter of interest, the only liquid having a stronger surface tension than water is the metal mercury, which is liquid under normal conditions.)

Perspiration produced by the body occurs in both liquid and vapor form. If the body wants to cool itself (and rid itself of some dissolved salts, waste and oils), it pushes some of its water out through the pores in the skin for evaporation and, in the process, evaporation creates a cooling effect for the skin.

Through exertion or extreme air temperatures and humidity, the warmer the body core becomes, the more moisture or perspiration is produced by the skin to help lower the body core temperature through evaporation. Sometimes the body gets overloaded by too much cooling demand and an extreme condition occurs, called "heat prostration" or "heat stroke". This is when the perspiration mechanism stops and the body core temperature rises dangerously. The other exception is when the body becomes dehydrated by too much moisture loss and the perspiration mechanism stops to preserve the remaining water supply in the body.

When evaporation takes place, heat is given off, cooling off the remaining liquid and the surface from which it is evaporated. It is true with our air conditioners at home, and it is true of our body.

When we add clothing to this equation, the rules change, depending upon the properties and nature of the fibers or materials that make them up as well as the design of the clothes themselves. However, there are some basics that do not change. There are several very important technical terms we must know and understand as we deal with moisture management. They are:

## ABSORBENCY -

The ability of a hydrophilic (water loving) to take water into itself, moving it through the actual structure of the fiber (and, in the case of cotton and wool, into a hollow or spongy core where it flows to the outside of the fiber) as well as over, along and around the fiber surface for evaporation. This is a property of natural fibers and some synthetics, such as acetate, rayon and, to a degree, nylon.

## ADSORBENCY -

The property of some water hating (hydrophobic) synthetic fibers to encourage water to flow along, around and over (but not through) the fibers to be carried away for evaporation. This process is generally called "wicking". If this property is not built (inherent) into the fiber,

# MOISTURE MANAGEMENT
# THE SIMPLE WICKING PROCESS

Moisture management is the process of moving excess moisture (perspiration) from the skin and transferring it away from the body in some manner or other for ultimate evaporation.

This process is accomplished by the use of **(a)** natural fibers (that are "water loving" or hydrophilic and absorb moisture into themselves and transfer it), and by **(b)** synthetic fibers (that are generally "water hating" or hydrophobic plastics) that have been chemically treated to break down the water surface tension and allow it to move along and around the fibers (wicking) away from the body for evaporation.

Cotton Fibers Absorbing

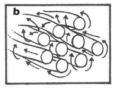

Synthetic Filaments Wicking

Other types of synthetic fibers, by their chemical and electrical nature, prevent most of the moisture from holding together in drops. These fibers keep moisture mostly in water vapor form for dissipation or allow moisture to freely move over and around the fibers for evaporation.

The knitted synthetic fabric illustrated has been treated with a "wicking agent" or chemical that **(c)** picks up the moisture from the skin, breaks down the water droplets and allows it to flow over, along and around the fibers (the "wicking action") to the fabric surface where it spreads out to evaporate. At the same time, **(d)** the body's water vapor is allowed to escape, helping to keep the wearer comfortable in warm or active conditions.

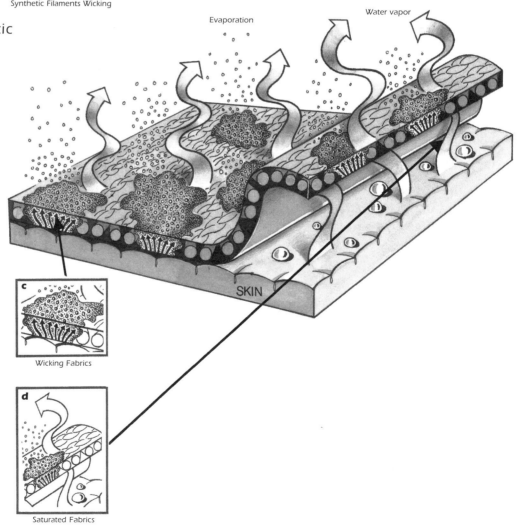

Evaporation

Water vapor

SKIN

Wicking Fabrics

Saturated Fabrics

some fibers can be chemically treated to enhance their "wicking" properties.

## Hydrophilic:

Literally, **"water loving"**. This term relates to all materials, fibers and finishes that readily absorb water or take water into the fiber or material itself. Nearly all natural fibers, protein (animal hair - wool, mohair, etc.) or cellulosic (vegetable fibers - cotton, linen, etc.) have this characteristic as do some synthetic fibers, such as rayon, acetate and, to a lesser degree, nylon.

## Hydrophobic:

Literally, **"water hating"**. This term relates to all materials, fibers and finishes that repel water and do not allow water to penetrate them. Most petroleum-based synthetic fibers fall into this group, including polyester, acrylic and polypropylene. (Nylon is mostly hydrophobic, but it does absorb more moisture than the other two fibers.) However, many of these fibers can be chemically modified to **transfer** moisture in one fashion or the other while polypropylene, the most hydrophobic of all fibers, is noted for its excellent inherent moisture transference characteristic.

## Wicking:

**The ability of a hydrophobic fiber to rapidly move moisture along channels around and along the fiber and the fabric structure, helping it to pass quickly through a fabric structure for moisture control and evaporation.** This property can be built into the fiber by its chemical and physical nature or it can be added to the fiber when it is created. Also, fabrics can be subjected to certain chemical treatments in dyeing and finishing that can enhance the fabric's ability to move, or "wick", moisture. Generally, the chemicals designed to assist this process interact with water molecules to disturb the water's natural characteristic to form a "surface tension" or molecular "skin", to form drops. Without that strong surface tension, water moves easily around and through the fiber and fabric structure to the fabric surface to be evaporated. (See Illustration page 72.) However, if this process happens too quickly, there can be a "refrigerating" or chilling effect, if the fabric gets saturated with moisture and evaporation takes place too fast.

## Moisture management by "ionization":

A relatively new approach to moisture management, chemical "ionization" of synthetic fabrics involves permanently placing a slight positive or negative electrical charge in a fabric. This results in the loss of liquid's "puddling" ability when it comes in contact with such a charged fabric and much of the water molecules stay in vapor state, passing through the fabric for easy dissipation in the air.

# MOISTURE MANAGEMENT- A "PUSH-PULL" CONTROL SYSTEM

This process is accomplished either by natural or absorbent synthetic fibers (rayon or acetate) taking moisture into themselves and transporting it to the air where it is evaporated. It is also accomplished by synthetic fibers that have natural or chemically altered "wicking" properties that allow water to be readily transported along, around and over the outer fiber surfaces to the fabric face, where it is spread out for evaporation.

This double faced, knitted fabric **(a)** combines two moisture management mechanisms (wickability and absorbency) to create an efficient moisture management system.

Two faced fabric - wicking bottom & absorbing top

Hydrophilic-the moisture goes through the fabric. Hydrophobic wicking layer the moisture goes around the fibers.

Evaporation

Water vapor

The skin side of the fabric is made of a wickable synthetic fiber that rapidly moves ("pushes") the moisture (perspiration) **(b)** away from the skin to the outer side of the fabric, made from an absorbent fiber (i.e.: cotton, rayon, etc.), that picks up ("pulls") the moisture up from the inner layer to spread

SKIN

Bottom wicking layer "pushes" & top absorbing layer "pulls"

out on the fabric surface for evaporation. The result is that the inside layer stays dry while the outer layer holds the moisture for evaporation (the "diaper" principle). The knitted fabric structure allows water vapor to escape **(c)**, adding to the comfort of this "push - pull" moisture management fabric system.

Water vapor escapes as well

(The rest of the moisture moves through the fabric with a capillary wicking action.)

**The "ionization" process results in less fabric saturation, faster drying and removes the need for the fabric to be in direct contact with the moisture source to work, as in wicking.**

## "Push - Pull" moisture management:

In this approach, two processes are happening separately and at the same time. In the classic "push-pull" system, the fabric in direct contact with the body is made of a naturally hydrophobic fiber that, by its nature or by having been treated in some manner or other, has a superior wicking characteristic. This part of the "system" picks up body moisture and quickly moves it ("pushes" it) from the body to the upper surface of the layer (or upper surface of the fabric, if two separate fabrics are involved) where it is picked up (pulled) by a second system of fibers that are highly hydrophilic. The inner layer of the system, next to the skin, stays relatively dry while the moisture saturates and spreads over the outer layer where the evaporation takes place. This is the same principle as the modern diaper that gets wet while keeping the baby dry. (See Illustration page 74.)

**Air temperature and humidity play an important role in mois-ture control. The problems of moisture management vary greatly winter to summer. In summertime, the warm air is generally light and is nearly always ready to pick up extra moisture from a damp surface except when the air is saturated with moisture with a high humidity and can't hold any more moisture. At that point, evaporation nearly ceases. Beginning in winter, the cold air is very dense and will not hold much moisture at all. Therefore, a fabric's ability to transmit moisture in VAPOR form in the cold months is vital to activewear comfort and performance. The waterproof, windproof, but breathable fabrics are no longer a luxury for winter performance - they are a necessity!**

Moisture management is certainly important in order for the active person to be comfortable and efficient in his or her physical pursuits. In the old days, it was enough to soak up the perspiration with a good old cotton or wool garment - but, today, thanks to careful research and product development, there are whole racks of wonderful products that can manage nearly any moisture management requirement and keep you comfortable and functioning at top performance levels, no matter what the conditions. Let's introduce you to many of them.

MOISTURE MANAGEMENT

# MOISTURE MANAGEMENT

## AKWATEK® / AKWADYNE®

There are more ways to manage moisture in synthetic fabrics for apparel than "wicking" alone. **Comfort Technologies' Akwatek®** process is one of them. This process places a minute electrical charge into the treated fabric that reacts with the water molecules of perspiration and interferes with the water's ability to form droplets and stay in liquid form. Moisture easily moves through the fabric to escape in the air. Result? The fabric does not saturate as in ordinary wicking moisture control. The "system" of moisture movement from the body to the air is self-controlling (the more you perspire, the more moisture is pushed out) and the fabric dries faster. (However, in very humid conditions, the efficiency of the process can be somewhat less efficient, as with the wicking process as well.) In cold conditions, the process is supposed to trap a warm layer of water vapor in the fabric to act as insulation. All kinds of activewear can be found using the process. Akwatek® is special to polyester fabrics and **Akwadyne®** is the ticket for nylon.

## BAGDAD

**Travis Textiles** offers this special nylon/polyester blend fabric to the technical sports apparel market featuring excellent abrasion characteristics plus the breathable, moisture management performance and fast drying of Comfort Technologies' Akwadyne® electrostatic moisture control process. Available now in shorts, shirts and technical sports apparel.

## BIO DRI®

**Nautilus** introduces a new, high performance, high tech fabric made with a special fiber blend that is reputed to assure maximum moisture management yet be durably anti-microbial to protect against development of odors from bacterial growth, fungus or mildew. Featuring a unique, treated blend of primarily cotton and a special acetate fiber, supported by stretch nylon, **Bio Dri®** is featured in workout clothes and socks and is designed to keep your "abs" and "pecs" comfortable, microbe-free and looking good.

## BREATHABLES®

**Gilda Marx** Incorporated offers a new lining fabric for its active bodywear and tights that features the moisture control of DuPont's Coolmax® fiber. This efficiently wicks away moisture through the outer fabric for evaporation and resists the development of bacteria and fungus that can cause infections.

## CAMBRELLE®

A leading non-woven shoe, boot or sneaker lining fabric from **Faytex Corp.**, **Cambrelle®** is made of 100% special bi-component nylon fibers, called Hetrofil nylon from DuPont U.K., that absorb three times their weight in moisture but dry quickly. This material is reputed to be very

74

breathable, resistant to odors and superior in strength, abrasion and pilling resistance, just the ticket for shoes and sneakers.

## CAPILENE®

Microdenier fibers are the secret behind **Patagonia's Capilene®** collection of performance underwear and lining fabrics that are said to be frictionless, adsorbent, yet fast drying with good thermal efficiency in both wet and dry conditions, breathable and anti-microbial to prevent odors and mildew. The weights and types of **Capilene®** fabrics range from "silk weight" through mid-weight, and even are brushed on both sides for the "expedition weight", depending on need, ranging from aerobics to mountain climbing, trekking and beyond.

## CMC®

**InSport** International has created a comfortable marriage of two of the "Kings of Comfort" - cotton and Coolmax® staple fiber from DuPont®. The result is a user-friendly fabric with a natural cotton face plus the superior moisture management of the cotton-like Coolmax® fibers next to the skin for performance comfort for the recreational athlete. Coolmax® pulls the moisture away from the skin and the cotton layer picks it up to move it out for controlled evaporation. Look for the **CMC®** labels on tops, tees, tanks and other clothes for walking, running, biking, lifting and aerobics.

## COMFORTEX®

**Charbert** offers a new collection of active outerwear or innerwear fabrics with superior moisture management that are specially treated with Comfort Technologies' Akwatek® (polyester) and Akwadyne® (nylon) hydrophilic finishes. These finishes are designed to create an electrostatic condition in the fibers that causes the rapid evaporation of the majority of perspiration generated by the body in exercise. It also allows moisture vapor to easily move through the fabric for efficient disbursement while the balance of the perspiration wicks for evaporation. Also, it is claimed, in colder conditions when evaporation is slower, a 'vapor barrier' of water vapor builds up in the fabric, creating an insulating and warming condition for the wearer.

## COTTONWIQUE®

For moisture management, **Coville**, Inc. offers **Cottonwique®** fabrics that are specially made with a soft layer of Fortrel® polyester next to the skin and an outer layer of cotton. The treated wicking characteristic of the polyester fibers moves body moisture away from the skin (without becoming saturated with water) and into the cotton layer, where the moisture is quickly absorbed and transported to the outer skin of the fabric for efficient evaporation. This moisture management process is called "push-pull", with the polyester pushing the moisture into the cotton and the cotton pulling the moisture away from the polyester. These fabrics are ideal for the intermediate layers of a total performance garment system or as a plain top, warmup, shorts, etc., for moderate weather conditions.

## DRICLIME®

**Marmot Mountain Ltd.** has created a family of unique bi-component knitted fabrics for garment linings and two weights of long underwear that demonstrate excellent moisture management and moderate insulation. When used for light aerobic wear, **Driclime®** is a two-faced circular knit fabric that is plaited to position one yarn on one side of a fabric and another yarn on the opposite side. Heavier, brushed continuous filament polyester fibers are on the inner side of the fabric for insulation while smaller spun yarns are on the outside of the fabric to assist and enhance the wicking action of the fabric. Driclime® fabric is also available in mid-weight and lightweight versions, both made with the two-faced circular knit with a special piqué construction for better stretch and moisture absorption. Trevira® ESP® stretch yarns are added to the mid-weight underwear version for better fit, flexibility and comfort.

## DRI F.I.T.®

**Nike, Inc.** checks in with their collection of "base layer fabrics" that are focused on comfort and excellent moisture management. Made of polyester microfibers, this fabric group consists of a variety of fabrics especially designed for specific sporting activities. They are engineered to quickly wick body moisture away from the athlete's skin, keeping him dry while moving the moisture to the fabric's surface where it can evaporate or be picked up by another fabric layer for further transport to evaporation. **Dri F.I.T.®** is available for running, training, soccer, cycling, golf and cold weather sports.

## DRILAYER™

This fabric from **Moving Comfort** is a two-ply construction of soft, hydrophobic polyester next to the skin and a quick drying nylon on the outside to create a "push-pull" moisture management system. The looped polyester inner knit works with the body's moisture production to "push" perspiration through to the surface layer where the treated nylon layer picks up the moisture and "pulls" it through to the fabric surface for rapid evaporation. This system is enhanced by the application of a special, durable wicking agent that is applied in fabric finishing. **DriLayer™'s** super wicking properties keep the body dry and can be used as a first layer or as an outer garment.

## DRI-LEX®

**Faytex** Corporation presents a high degree of comfort and performance in shoe and boot linings with the special **Dri-Lex®** bi-component fabric structures. These combine the superior moisture management performance of Allied Signal's Hydrofil® **MVT** (**M**oisture **V**apor **T**ransport) nylon to absorb foot perspiration while the special dry-faced knitted natural foam-backed laminate fabric stays soft, cool and dry against the foot. Depending upon the construction and design, the linings can range from sueded to a piqué textured face and may feature a Ban-O-Dor® anti-microbial treatment to retard bacterial development.

## DRI-LEX® AERO-SPACER™

This is more sophisticated version of **Faytex** Corp.'s Dri-Lex® boot lining laminated fabric collection. A unique tri-laminate fabric structure features a specially designed moisture management cushioned 'air chamber' as the middle layer in the sandwich of fabrics, made of Allied Signal's Hydrofil® nylon. This layer is reputed to ventilate and cool the foot. With a micromesh hydrophilic lining and a moisture transport layer next to the shell material, the **Dri-Lex® Aero-Spacer™** system is truly a performance moisture management fabric.

## DRI-LEX® FLEECE

This time **Faytex** Corp. has created a shoe and boot liner fabric where the skin-side of the fabric is a brushed fleece knit made from Allied Signal's Hydrofil® nylon laminated to another hydrophilic layer of nylon to draw moisture away from the skin. It is reputed to be the only truly "stay-dry"

fleece lining for shoes and boots in the business.

## DRYLINE®

**Dryline®** is a special moisture management fabric from **Milliken & Co.** that employs the principle of "push - pull" to create a condition whereby the wearer stays comfortable and dry. The perspiration is transported rapidly from a hydrophobic (water hating), but highly wickable, brushed inner layer of the fabric to a highly absorbent, hydrophilic (water loving) or highly wickable, but hydrophobic, outer layer for evaporation. The outer layer of this dual component knitted fabric is made of a specially treated, super-absorbent nylon that adds to the abrasion resistance of the fabric in rugged use. The fabric is light in weight and suitable for running gear and other performance outerwear applications.

## DRYLINER®

This is circular knitted bra liner fabric that has the warmth and friendly feel of cotton, but is actually a blend of DuPont's Coolmax® moisture management polyester and Lycra® spandex for comfort and fit. **InSport** is the source for **Dryliner®** fabrics and they have engineered the fabric to have exceptional horizontal stretch characteristics with inhibited and controllable vertical stretch for ideal support in bra applications. Used as a liner in all sorts of aerobic, fitness as well as sports bras.

# MOISTURE MANAGEMENT

## DRYSPORT®

**InSport** has developed this two-faced fabric that offers superior abrasion and wear resistant nylon on one side and the super softness of DuPont's Micromattique® microfiber on the inside. This provides good wicking action to comfortably transport moisture to the outer face, creating the classic "push-pull" moisture management scenario to keep the wearer nice and dry. **Drysport®** is in InSport's top-of-the-line cycling shorts, mountain biking gear and bibs.

## DRYWICK™

**adidas America** presents a moisture management fabric with a special knitted texture look that proves to be functional, as well. Constructed with soft, wickable spun polyester yarns, this lightweight fabric is knitted with a bold piqué stitch on the surface of the fabric that offers more surface area for evaporation of perspiration to take place during exercise. Visa® is the moisture management secret weapon in **Drywick™**. It makes the perfect inside "comfort" layer for a WPB shell system or can be by itself in moderate weather to help keep you comfortable.

## FIELDSENSOR®

**Fieldsensor®** is a high performance, moisture management bi-laminate knitted fabric from **Toray** that relies on the "push-pull" wicking technique whereby the inner layer has excellent wicking properties, but absorbs no moisture (hydrophobic) and the bonded outer layer is specially engi-

neered to handle much more moisture than the inner layer. This layer rapidly "pulls" away the moisture from the skin and "pushes" it into the outer fabric structure where it is quickly spread over the surface of the fabric for evaporation, "pulling" more moisture out of the system for evaporation. The skin stays relatively dry, no matter how strenuous the exercise gets. Toray offers this double layer product for biking, tennis, fitness or as a lining for snowboarding or skiing garments.

## HYDRASUEDE®

If softness, excellent moisture management and stretch performance and control are on your fabric "wish list", you should consider **InSport's Hydrasuede®** support fabrics. This exclusive blend not only gives the wearer the soft, cottony feel of DuPont's Supplex® and its high performance, but also the "give-and-go" stretch comfort and control of Lycra® spandex. Especially sueded for extra 'peach skin' softness, Hydrasuede® is treated with a durable moisture management finish that enhances the perspiration control of the fabric for added comfort in fast drying. All of this is keyed to women's fitness apparel, including shorts, bras, running tights, cycling shorts, etc.

## HYDROMOVE®

**Reebok International, Ltd.** introduces a new collection of high-tech, moisture management fabrics for multi-sport, running, cross training, fitness, team sports and cycling utilizing Hydromove™ technology. Instead of purely wicking moisture through the fabric, like treated synthetics, or absorbing it into the fiber, like cotton, **Hydromove®** fabrics are specially processed to utilize unique hydrophilic sites along hydrophobic fibers. These attract moisture molecules and break them apart, making it difficult for water to stay in liquid form. Most of it remains in vapor form, allowing it to easily pass through the fabric for dissipation and evaporation. The result is an all-season, self-regulating moisture management control system. (The more you perspire, the faster the system works; the less you sweat, the slower the moisture transfer.) It is not even necessary for the treated fabric to touch the skin to work. In cool conditions, Hydromove® fabrics claim to help trap body heat, maintaining warmth and comfort for the wearer.

## INTERA®

**Intera®** by Intera is a special process designed to permanently bond special hydrophilic (water loving) molecules to the surface of a wide variety of synthetic fibers (especially nylon). This allows them to efficiently transport (wick) moisture along and around the fiber's continuous filaments or staples, helping to keep the wearer comfortable and dry in most conditions. In addition, because it promotes rapid drying, Intera® does not allow bacteria, yeast or mildew (that require moist conditions to flour-

ish) to develop on the treated synthetic fibers. Intera® is quite durable and stands up to repeated washing and cleanings, is reputed to resist soil build-up in treated fibers and oily stains are supposed to wash out easily.

## LIFA® ACTIVE

For top-of-the-line performance in functional underwear, **Helly-Hansen** nominates **Lifa® Active**. Made with a special combination of three different fibers in a unique knitted fabric structure, each component serves a definite and vital role in this underwear fabric's success. The fabric contains spun polypropylene for superior moisture transport and lightweight insulation; fast-drying cotton for absorbent, insulating comfort and friendly feel; and continuous-filament polyamide (nylon) for strength and recovery. Put them all together in the right combination and you have a very impressive performance underwear fabric system for cross country or downhill skiing, backpacking and those other challenging activities.

## LIFA® ATHLETIC

The Lifa® fabric systems from **Helly-Hansen** are designed to balance moisture management and insulation, depending upon the specific end use. **Lifa® Athletic** is designed to provide superior moisture management and breathability in skin fitting garments. The system uses a special combination of a knitted construction with both channels and holes, called

# MOISTURE MANAGEMENT

Ultra, and a very fine staple polypropylene spun yarn, called Prolite 5000. An open, breathable fabric structure is created with very wickable fibers to carry away large amounts of perspiration in heavy exercise without getting saturated and heavy. Look for it in performance underwear.

## LOOPKNIT™

**Loopknit™**is the trademark that **Monterey Mills** has chosen for their new, lightweight, loop textured knit fabric created using their proprietary, specialized equipment and knitting machine attachments. Available in an array of spun fibers (polyester, acrylic or wool), these fabrics not only look good, they have exceptional drapability, wicking and warmth without weight as well as having great strength and easy care properties. Here is performance and fashion in one package for performance outerwear and sportswear.

## M.C.S.®

Standing for "**M**oisture **C**ontrol **S**ystem", **Burlington Performance Fabrics** offers their top moisture management fabrics made of hydrophobic (water hating) nylon or microfiber polyester. These fabrics are treated to be permanently and durably hydrophilic (water loving) to quickly wick away moisture from the skin by spreading it out over the fiber surfaces to assist quick drying. This process keeps the athlete more comfortable and dryer even during strenuous activities. Look for the tags on technical sportswear, travel wear, trekking and backpacking.

## MAX™

Take a fine 100% nylon fiber and position it on the fabric face and place under it DuPont's CoolMax™ moisture management fiber and you have created a technical fabric that moves moisture away from the body for efficient evaporation and comfort performance. **Consoltex, Inc.** presents **Max™**, a fabric for all seasons - as a lightweight shell fabric for biking or golf in mild weather and as a great moisture management lining under any performance shell fabric system in winter for skiing, snowboarding, etc.

## NATUREXX®

A collection of special nylon and Lycra® spandex fabrics from **Darlington** features the Intera® permanent moisture management process for nylon, offering not only excellent wicking properties, but also anti-microbial protection against the growth of odor-causing bacteria, fungi and mildew. Intera® also offers a superior soil and stain release protection to keep colors bright and clean. Created in various weights, lusters and bright colors, the **Naturexx®** collection of fabrics can range from modest comfort support to compression-certified fabrics under the DuPont Lycra® Power program. Look for them in swimwear, athletic performance wear, compression garments and intimate apparel.

# MOISTURE MANAGEMENT

## PHIN-TECH™

This fabric is a good candidate for the clothing layer you put on first before you pile on the heavier performance outerwear. **Pearl Izumi** has developed a special, textured polyolefin (polypropylene) knitted fabric that is totally hydrophobic, yet has excellent moisture wicking properties as well as an extremely low thermal conductivity that conserves some body heat. Because polyolefin is the lightest of all synthetic fibers and does not absorb any moisture, the fabric stays lightweight and relatively dry, no matter how hard you exercise. Constructed in a 1x1 rib, the fabric is body hugging and ideal for underwear and bodywear applications.

## POLARTEC 100 SERIES BI-POLAR

**Malden Mills** has taken the performance properties of the excellent 100 Series product and created a two-sided fabric made from special micro fibers: one side picks up moisture from the skin and "moves" (wicks) it up to the outer layer where it is spread out for quick evaporation. This is called a "push-pull" moisture management system. In addition, the **Polartec 100 Series Bi-Polar** is anti-microbial and breathable, allowing water vapor to easily escape the fabric. Look for it in underwear, bike jerseys and performance shirting.

## QUICK WICK™

**Summit Knitting Mills** presents its proprietary performance chemical process that imparts superior wicking characteristics and moisture management to a broad range of synthetic fibers, including nylon, polyester and acrylic, used in knitted fabrics destined for the activewear and team sports markets. The proprietary process forms a physical polymer graft on the host fiber, resulting in a dramatic and rapid 360° increase in the liquid surface area from the point the moisture reaches the fabric surface. This results in rapid drying of the garment and enhanced comfort to the wearer. Not only is **Quick Wick**™efficient in moisture management, it is super soft and has excellent soil release properties. Current fabrics in the Quick Wick™ collection feature nylon and acrylic constructions.

## RADIATOR®
## COLLECTION:

The **Radiator® Collection** is a special group of fabrics from **Russell Athletic** that features an excellent "push-pull" moisture control approach by combining DuPont's CoolMax® moisture management fiber and cotton. The CoolMax® yarn, which does not absorb moisture, is positioned in the knitted structure on the inside face of the fabric, where it quickly picks up body moisture and transfers it to the outer, extremely absorbent cotton face yarns where the moisture is evaporated in a controlled manner. The wearer stays dry and warm, no matter how hard he or she exercises.

# MOISTURE MANAGEMENT

These high performance team sport and workout apparel garments are available today, ready to keep you comfortable.

## SCHOELLER® - dryskin

Here is a new lightweight stretch woven fabric from **Schoeller®**, called **"dryskin"**, that features a tough outer shell of polyamide (nylon) and Cordura® Plus from DuPont and its special four-channel cross-section fiber, CoolMax®, on the back side of the fabric. This greatly increases the evaporation surface of the fiber, allowing it to dry faster and move moisture more rapidly. The addition of Lycra® spandex gives the fabric flexibility and recovery, while its efficient moisture transport makes it an excellent choice for mountain climbing, cross country skiing, biking, trekking and other activities that induce heavy perspiration. It is claimed that it keeps the skin dry even after hours of intensive sports activities.

## SCHOELLER®- dynamic & dynamic Extreme

This tough-wearing, stretch-woven fabric is designed for multi-purpose applications ranging from sports to athleisure wear year round. It is highly elastic (thanks to Lycra® spandex), breathable and very durable (thanks to Cordura® nylon), and capable of being dyed with the brightest fashion colors. Other products, such as **"dynamic®"** and the heavier **"dynamic® Extreme"**, are just the ticket for mountaineering, skiing, cycling, hiking pants, jackets, overalls, suits, etc.

## SYNCHILLA®

The name of the game with **Patagonia's Synchilla®** is warmth without weight. Made with Wellman's EcoSpun® recycled polyester, this double-brushed, two-faced fleece fabric is breathable, has good moisture management properties, is quick drying and very easy care - but, most importantly, it is an excellent insulator. The fabric is intended to be part of a total system of fabrics and garments that are designed to be used together to keep you alive and well in extreme situations, but can be worn comfortably in less trying conditions. You'll find **Synchilla®** as an 'under-top' or such garment that insulates with little bulk.

## T3®

This is family of garments from **Moving Comfort** that uses technical wicking fabrics exclusively in all layers. These garments afford the athlete maximum moisture management. **T3**™ fabrics include any one or more of the following: DuPont's CoolMax®, Deer Creek Fabric's Polywick®- treated fabrics and Intera® - treated fabrics such as Intera® mesh and Intera® poly/Lycra® jersey.

## TACTEL® AQUATOR

Tactel® Aquator is a two-sided fabric designed to wick moisture away from the skin. There are two versions of this product: **Aquator®** for comfort and **Tactel®** for performance. The "comfort" version features an inner layer of Tactel® fiber from **DuPont** and an outer layer of cotton, wool or viscose (rayon) and is great for golf shirts, intimates and ready-to-wear. The "performance" version features two layers of 100% Tactel® or a combination of Tactel® and polyester for high performance activities. In both systems, the Tactel® layer wicks the moisture to the outer surface where it is spread over a large area for evaporation, keeping you dry and comfortable in leisure or in sport activities.

## ULTRASENSOR®

**Pearl Izumi** has developed a family of high performance moisture management fabrics that feature the "push-pull" moisture transfer method to keep the wearer as dry as possible while cycling, running or in other aerobic or training sports activities. This is done by knitting a double-faced fabric, placing heavier filament polyester fibers on the skin side of the fabric and very fine polyester microfibers on the outside of the fabric structure. The effect is to have the outer fibers "pull" the moisture away from the coarser inner fibers, evaporate it and keep the subject dry. **Ultrasensor®** fabrics range from a lightweight mesh, to a spandex-containing fabric for shorts and tights, to the Kodiak® style for Fall/Winter in a heavier weight fabric.

## WINNING COMFORT®

A well established trademark from **Liberty Fabrics**, **Winning Comfort®** is a trademark that can be found on a broad range of performance polyester and Lycra® spandex fibers blended into warp knitted and circular knitted fabrics designed for the activewear markets. This fabric collection not only offers the comfort, support and fit found in spandex-containing fabrics, but also added moisture management properties due to a special finish that greatly improves the wicking characteristics of the fabrics as well as their soil-release properties (especially releasing oil-borne stains). Available in both single-faced and two-faced fabrics, you too can have Winning Comfort® in cycling and running gear, skiwear, sports underwear, soccer uniforms, etc.

## YUKON LIGHTS®

Here is a lighter version of Yukon 2000 from **Huntingdon**. This one is napped on one side only for lining applications and on both sides for underwear and lightweight casual performance wear. **Yukon Lights®** is reputed to have excellent moisture management characteristics utilizing the same "push - pull" system as its "Big Brother", thanks to the napped polyester fiber content on face and back.

# A
# TECHNOLOGICAL
# REVOLUTION

Certainly, one of the most exciting developments in the performance apparel "revolution" is the evolution of the concept of having one fabric and garment system addressing three problems at once - water, wind and "breathability".

## WATER,
## WIND AND
## BREATHABILITY

# WATERPROOF AND WINDPROOF, BUT BREATHABLE

## STAYING DRY AND COMFORTABLE IN THE WORST OF CONDITIONS

**The art of staying dry and comfortable in extreme conditions is being addressed today by a broad range of performance shell fabric systems.** Water repellency can be accomplished by applying a variety of chemical finishes, which are called **DWR** (**D**urably **W**ater **R**esistant), to outer shell fabrics. Some of these coatings need to be reapplied periodically to maintain their maximum performance levels. The **WPB** (**W**ater**P**roof/**B**reathable) revolution started 20 years ago with the introduction of permeable membrane technology that, when applied to a shell fabric system, made it waterproof, yet allowed moisture (water) vapor and excess heat to escape the garment system while keeping it effectively windproof.

Today, from golfing to hiking, cycling to climbing, from yachting to jogging, there are several **WPB** (add windproof) approaches available to accomplish varying degrees of each of these goals, depending upon the wearer's needs:

■ **The lamination and bonding of a permeable hydrophobic (water hating) membrane or film** to a densely woven shell fabric that will still allow moisture vapor and excess heat to escape.

■ **The application of a permeable hydrophobic coating** (applied on the fabric surface) that is spread on the back of a tightly woven shell fabric that will still allow moisture vapor and excess heat to escape.

■ **The application of a non-porous (monolithic), but water loving coating to one or more fabric layers that allows controlled "breathability".** Sometimes, special, very tiny ceramic beads are used to coat the fabric to better control the waterproof/breathable nature of the coating.

■ **A very finely woven fabric made from microfiber yarns that are so tightly constructed and packed in that the tiny gaps in the fabric are smaller than rain drops,** but allow moisture vapor and excess heat to escape while staying windproof.

To check on the degree of "breathability", check the fabric's **MVTR rating** (**M**oisture **V**apor **T**ransfer **R**ate). The higher the MVTR rating number, the more "breathable" the fabric.

WATERPROOF AND WINDPROOF, BUT BREATHABLE

# WATERPROOF AND WINDPROOF, BUT BREATHABLE

Introduced over 20 years ago by W.L. Gore & Associates, Inc. and marketed under the "**Gore-Tex®**" trademark, this patented product captured the imagination of the industry. Today, there is a whole "universe" of W.L. Gore & Associates' products out there together with a new generation of **WPB** (**W**ater**P**roof, **B**reathable) products ready and willing to keep you dry, warm and comfortable. However, before we discuss combined approaches to accomplish multiple protection and performance factors, we should examine one of the most important protection elements of all - water penetration resistance.

**In reviewing the techniques that are being used to accomplish water penetration protection, among other things, we must ask basic questions about the fibers and fabrics involved, the weather conditions, the type and intensity of the activity involved and the garment "system" being employed, if any.**

The water resistance of a fabric depends upon several factors. As an example, the fiber content of a fabric surface is very important. Is it water hating or water loving or has it been treated in some manner to be more one than the other?) Also, how hard and heavy is it raining? Is it raining straight down or is it wind-driven? How porous or open is the fabric structure being rained on? Has a "second line of defense" against water penetration been built into the fabric

or garment system using "barrier" material like a coating, membrane, film, etc.? All of these factors will play a part in finding the "waterproof" solution to the equation.

Of course, there is nothing new about trying to make clothing water resistant or totally waterproof. In fact, next to insulation, this was probably one of the first performance aspects of clothing early man worked on. One of the earliest methods to get rid of water on clothing was to coat the garment with fat or grease and to create long fringes on key areas of tanned skin garments (buckskins) that would act as "drain pipes" for rainwater, quickly carrying it off the garment surface. The fringes didn't keep the garment waterproof, but they guaranteed that the garment would dry faster after the rain and wouldn't allow water to collect to evaporate too quickly and chill the wearer.

In the case of wovens and, later, knitted fabrics, an early solution was to apply some sort of water resistant coating to the fabric face. Originally, materials such as waxes, varnishes or oils were used to fill up the tiny holes in the weave of the garments. This worked pretty well, but the fabrics ended up heavy and stiff and did not "breathe" very well. Even though you didn't get wet, your own condensed perspiration inside the garment kept you damp anyway. When vulcanized rubber came along, fabrics were coated with it for rain protection and,

# WATERPROOF, WINDPROOF BUT BREATHABLE - A BREATHABLE HYDROPHOBIC MEMBRANE BARRIER TRI-LAMINATE

**A waterproof, windproof but breathable fabric system is created by bonding a breathable but weather-impervious membrane barrier to a fabric system with such tiny holes that wind and the smallest rain drop cannot penetrate it. Yet this fabric is nonetheless porous enough to allow water vapor and heat to escape into the air, keeping the wearer dry and comfortable. Garments made of such fabrics are usually outer shells worn along with garments that offer insulation and/or moisture management features.**

This fabric system is a tri-laminate (having three layers bonded together). The outer layer **(a)** is a tightly woven, synthetic shell fabric that is tough and water and wind resistant in light conditions. However, in heavier wind and rain or snow conditions, both wind and water can penetrate the fabric structure.

Outer layer resistant but not totally wind & waterproof

Water vapor

Excess heat

WIND

Hydrophobic micro porous membrane

The middle layer **(b)** is made of a micro-thin, water hating (hydrophobic) membrane that is bonded directly to the inside of the shell fabric. The membrane has millions of tiny holes that are so small they will not allow the finest water droplets or heat-sapping winds from penetrating the fabric. However, excess water vapor and heat can easily pass through the fabric for dissipation, keeping the wearer dry and comfortable.

Breathable, micro porus membrane bonded between layers

Insulating brushed fabric

Skin

SKIN

The bonded inner layer **(c)** is a light weight, brushed knitted fabric that is designed to add softness and a bit of insulation to the overall fabric system.

Insulating inner layer yet releases excess heat & water vapor

90

although they were totally waterproof and more permanent, the condensation and weight problems increased.

After WWII, when plastics became available, a lot of wet weather garments were made directly from plastic sheets or plastic films and were bonded to textiles to create rainproof clothing. They were totally rainproof - but, next to these garments, the old "oil skins" were comfortable! Although much lighter, there was absolutely no escape for the condensed moisture in these garment systems and the wearer literally "stewed" in his or her own juices.

**Chemical treatments and coatings to "waterproof" the outer or "shell" fabrics and or the garments themselves, have been an available and workable approach to rain protection for many years. These finishes can be applied in the dyeing and finishing process, added to the fabric later by being sprayed or spread on the fabric and "cured" after it is finished, or applied to the finished garment in some sort of dry cleaning process.**

The best of these treatments work quite well to keep out the rain, although few, if any, are totally waterproof. Others only keep light rain and drizzle from penetrating the garments. However, many of the best of these treatments tend to experience durability problems in wear and care and must be re-applied periodi-

cally in some manner or other during the life of the garment. Some of the best chemical waterproofing treatments qualify to be termed **DWR** or **D**urably **W**ater **R**esistant and we will be listing them here.

The **WPB (W**ater**P**roof/**B**reathable) approach to waterproof protection had to wait until the 1980's when certain ultra-thin, micro-porous synthetic films and membranes, breathable coatings and microfibers were developed. Today, new elasticized WPB films and membranes are being introduced as well as new breathable coating approaches, adding new dimensions to the three existing miracles - waterproof, windproof, breathable. (And now, four-way stretch built-in! What next?)

However, before we review the current approaches to WPB (and windproofing), we need to re-examine the properties of water. When we addressed "Moisture Management" we spent considerable time talking about the strength of the "surface tension" of water and how it must be dealt with in order to move moisture through, along and around fibers and fabric structures. This same property causes water to "clump" together in raindrops or droplets that are about the size of 100 microns (1 micron = 1,000th of a millimeter). Most tightly woven shell fabrics have tiny gaps in the weave that are even smaller.

# WATERPROOF, WINDPROOF BUT BREATHABLE
# A BREATHABLE, HYDROPHOBIC, BI-LAMINATE COATING SYSTEM

A waterproof, windproof but breathable fabric system is created by bonding a breathable but weather-impervious coating barrier to a fabric system with such tiny holes that wind and the smallest rain drop cannot penetrate it. Yet this fabric is nonetheless porous enough to allow vapor and heat to escape into the air, keeping the wearer dry and comfortable. Garments made of such fabrics are seldom used alone, but rather in combination with other insulating and/or moisture management layers of apparel.

This fabric is a bi-laminate (two layers bonded together) that features a tightly woven synthetic shell fabric that is somewhat wind and water resistant, but not in very wet and windy conditions. Some moisture is shown being driven into the weave structure of the surface fabric **(a)**. On the back of the fabric there is very thin, bonded coating that is made of a special hydrophobic (water hating), micro-porous material **(b)**

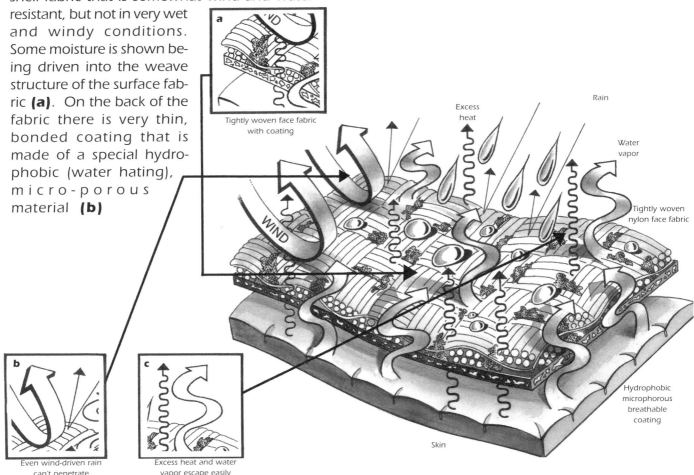

**a** Tightly woven face fabric with coating

**b** Even wind-driven rain can't penetrate

**c** Excess heat and water vapor escape easily

Rain

Excess heat

Water vapor

Tightly woven nylon face fabric

WIND

Hydrophobic microphorous breathable coating

Skin

that will not permit water or heat-robbing wind to penetrate the fabric system. This allows the extremely fine water droplets of water vapor to escape together with excess heat **(c)**, keeping the wearer dry and comfortable.

92

# WATERPROOF AND WINDPROOF, BUT BREATHABLE

**When rain hits the surface of a fabric that has no water repellent treatment, the pressure of the water drops hitting the fabric can drive them and the water already lying on the surface into the fabric structure and saturate it.**

By this time it should be obvious that hydrophilic fibers, such as cotton or wool, should not be selected as shell fabric fibers for "waterproof" performance apparel. (These fibers will still remain the fibers of choice for tailored raincoats, treated with good DWR finishes, where long exposure to the severe elements is rare. However, no matter what the DWR treatment on these fibers, in severe conditions, they will take in and hold moisture that can cause a chilling effect and increased weight, even if there is little or no actual water penetration.) Therefore, the fibers of choice for performance shell fabric applications are nylon and polyester, which are quite hydrophobic (water hating) by nature. These fibers usually have had some type of DWR application just to make sure there is the least amount of water penetration through the fabric structure, no matter how tightly woven it is or how hard it rains.

The latest approaches to waterproofing are:

- **The lamination and bonding of a permeable, hydrophobic membrane** (it has millions of minute holes or "pores" built into it that are much smaller than raindrops) to the inside surface of a fabric or between two separate layers of fabric. This membrane is very effective in preventing water and wind penetration while allowing water vapor and excess heat to escape. (See Illustration page 92)

- **Application of a permeable, hydrophobic coating** (with tiny pores built in ) to a fabric layer or layers, as in a bi or tri-laminate. This coating may or may not have stretchable characteristics to impart a comfort stretch character to the laminate. (See Illustration page 94)

- **Application of a "monolithic" or non-porous, but hydrophilic, coating to one or more fabric layers** that allows controlled "breathability" (in a molecular transfer process form) while keeping wind and rain out. (Sometimes, a special coating of microfine ceramics is added to this system to adjust the gap sizes in the coating and result in added performance.)

- **Weaving a fabric made from microfiber** that is so fine, tightly woven and dense that it will not allow in any wind or rain to penetrate it, yet it will allow water vapor to escape. (It may or may not be treated with a DWR finish.)

As you recall, a raindrop is 100 microns in size. In the cases of the

# WATERPROOF AND WINDPROOF, BUT BREATHABLE

porous membranes and the porous coatings, the pores are between 5 and 10 microns in size, while water vapor is 0.0004 microns in size. That is why fabrics coated or bonded with these products keep out any rain while allowing excess body heat to vent and water vapor to escape for evaporation. This is called "breathability". The other approaches work in slightly different ways, but they also allow these fabric systems to "breathe" while staying dry. **Note:** In order to tell the "breathability" of a product, ask the supplier for the product's **MVTR rating** [**M**oisture **V**apor **T**ransfer **R**ate]. The higher the rating number, the more "breathable" the fabric.

Wind resistance goes hand in hand with waterproofness. Wind penetration into a garment, whether through the tiny holes in the fabric structure or through the garment openings themselves, can and does contribute greatly to the body's ability to retain heat. **If the gaps in the garment are sealed against water, they are certainly sealed from wind penetration. Therefore, WPB fabrics could have another "W" added to represent "windproof" as well.**

When selecting a WPB garment, the best choice will always be **"The one that will best serve MY needs",** whether mountain climbing, skiing, back packing, snowboarding, golfing, biking or just "power" walking.

**All of these products are technological wonders and each deserves your consideration in finding the right level of performance and comfort in your apparel selection. Let's see what's out there for you in this technological revolution and what your choices will be.**

# WATERPROOF AND WINDPROOF, BUT BREATHABLE

## ACTIVENT®

**W. L. Gore & Associates, Inc.** offers a lightweight, two-layer fabric, branded **Activent®**, that is specially designed for high aerobic sports such as running, cycling, climbing, alpine and cross country skiing. Consisting of an ultra-thin composite membrane bonded to nylon or polyester fabrics, the fabric is windproof, extremely breathable and water resistant. Very lightweight and packable, Activent® fabrics are ideal for maintaining comfort in cold, windy conditions where light precipitation could dampen your spirits.

## amFIB™

The highest of the "High-Tech" fabrics offered by **Pearl Izumi, amFIB™** is a tri-laminate shell fabric that is light in weight yet offers wind and water protection while remaining breathable. The outer fabric layer is a tough, lightweight rip-stop fabric that has had spandex stretch added for two-way stretch comfort and aerodynamic fit. The middle layer is a special hydrophobic polyurethane laminate that holds the three fabrics together and keeps wind and water out while being extremely permeable to water vapor for breathability. The inside layer is made of a brushed, durable, hydrophobic fabric that adds comfort for the wearer. This three layer shell fabric system is light enough for running and cycling gear,

rainwear and other outdoor wear for most conditions.

## AQUAGUARD®

**Rotofil** presents a water and windproof fabric that breathes, thanks to a special hydrophobic, microporous polyurethane coating that is applied to its fabrics for performance wear. Such fabrics are typically used in outerwear as a shell fabric or as an intermediate layer in a performance garment system that protects while allowing water vapor to escape for added comfort.

## BURLINGTON COMPOSITE TECHNOLOGY®

The newest of **Burlington Performance Fabrics'** "performance fabric" offerings, **BURLINGTON COMPOSITE TECHNOLOGY®** is their name for a broad range of waterproof/breathable shell fabric systems. They range from a two-layer laminate combining a breathable membrane with the microfiber shell fabrics in a golf rainwear-weight to more robust tri-laminate shell fabrics for skiing featuring an interior layer of tricot fabric bonded to the breathable membrane and the dense outer shell. They will also be found in snowboarding gear and technical outerwear.

WATERPROOF AND WINDPROOF, BUT BREATHABLE

# WATERPROOF AND WINDPROOF, BUT BREATHABLE

## CALTECH®

When you hear the name, **Caltech®**, it says "technical" and "advanced". **Unitika America** has developed a family of special technically advanced fabrics carrying the name with performance coatings to address various outdoor problems for clothing. They all have various water resistance, wind resistance and breathability characteristics, depending on primary need. As example, **Caltech® R** emphasizes a high level of water "repellency" as well as moisture vapor permeability (breathability), a soft touch and is lightweight. **Caltech® SS** features a new coating technology that has high water resistance and windproofness. Maximum protection from wind-driven rain and water is **Caltech® HI's** coating that breathes but is "high" performance in wet conditions. All the coatings are also reputed to be very durable and are especially for outdoor wear and sportswear.

## CANARI THERMO FLEECE

**Canari Cycle Wear** has an exclusive **Thermo-Fleece** fabric for biking and almost any outdoor wear. It is a triple layer construction that is designed to protect you from the severe cold, wind and rain. The outer shell is made of DuPont nylon and Lycra® spandex, which is laminated to a Vapex® polyester film that is windproof and wa-

ter resistant, but breathable, and an inner layer of wickable polyester fleece for insulation, warmth and comfort. The total fabric system keeps you warm and dry and, no matter how hard you pedal uphill, your Thermo-Fleece cycling gear keeps on breathing and keeps you dry.

## CLIMA F.I.T.®

A very densely woven fabric construction, combined with the extreme fineness and coverage offered by microfibers, allows **Nike's Clima F.I.T.®** fabric to be highly water resistant, windproof, breathable and lightweight without coatings, laminates or finishes. The fabric structure is so dense that water droplets, even under pressure, have a hard time penetrating the fabric; yet the body's water vapor easily moves through the fibers and weave for evaporation, preventing moisture from condensing on the interior fabric face, making the athlete "clammy" and uncomfortable. Used in moderate conditions as a shell fabric or over another layer or two in extreme conditions, **Clima F.I.T.®** is intended for multiple sports including running, cycling, skating, skiing, golf and aerobic training.

## CLIMAGUARD®

**Climaguard®** is a trademark of **Rotofil** that is found on wind and water resistant (breathable), soft shell fabrics made of micro fibers. These

fabrics are said to be very tightly woven and, combined with the excellent, ultra-fine coverage of microfibers that fill in the gaps in the woven structure, the fabrics achieve their performance without coatings, films or membranes. These fabrics are used for lightweight shell fabric applications (wind jackets for golf, sailing, jogging, wind-breakers, etc.) or as the shell fabrics for insulated jackets and heavier weather gear.

## COMFORMAX® IB & IB STRETCH

A new approach to windproofness from **DuPont**, **ComforMax® IB** is a high performance lining fabric that offers a maximum of wind resistance as well as breathability and vapor transfer without the use of membrane technology and with minimum bulkiness. Using water-entangled polyolefin microfibers, the resulting fiber mat is remarkably thin, soft and pliable and marries well with all types of shell and lining fabrics without fiber migration. It is also available reinforced with Lycra® spandex for stretch, recovery and greater comfort in active applications.

## DARLEXX®

**Darlington Fabrics Corp.'s Darlexx®** fabrics are a family of laminates made from Darlington's warp knit elastic fabrics and a proprietary, hydrophilic (water loving), thermo-plastic (heat settable) film. The fabric and the film are permanently "married" or bonded together in a special way that carefully controls the tension of both the fabric and the film. This technology produces a remarkable (and patented), waterproof, breathable and windproof fabric collection that has four-way, "omni-directional" stretch performance. They are also very durable and easy care. There are **Darlexx®** fabrics that have a very smooth and "dragless" face for speed sports while others are made with microfibers that offer super softness and insulation. These fabrics are ideal for cycling, scuba, hiking, kayaking, running and all sorts of performance challenges.

## DERMIZAX®

High performance/high-tech are the proper terms for **Toray's** latest high end activewear **Dermizax®** fabric system. The secret to the fabric's exceptional performance is the ultra-thin, nonporous, hydrophobic membrane that is highly waterproof, even during strenuous wearer movement. At the same time, the membrane is stretchable and easily adjusts to movement without affecting the waterproof and breathable character of the fabric or weakening the "peeling strength" of the membrane bond. Toray calls it "Shape Memory". The bonded membrane has exceptional moisture vapor per-

WATERPROOF AND WINDPROOF, BUT BREATHABLE

# WATERPROOF AND WINDPROOF, BUT BREATHABLE

meability for superior breathability and minimizes the condensation of perspiration on the fabric's inner layer. The system is available in a variety of shell fabrics including a microfiber woven shell fabric. This one can go mountain climbing with you or on that ocean yacht race as your "wet gear" or just for snowboarding or skiing and you'll stay dry and comfortable.

## DERMOFLEX®

When it comes to championship winter weather, Canada is up there with the best of them! **Consoltex Inc.** from Canada offers hard wearing, water and snowproof fabrics that have special waterproof, windproof and breathable coating that keeps the weather where it belongs - away from you. Thanks to the micro-porous coating, this tough shell fabric could be the perfect outer layer when you snowboard, ski or snowshoe over to the curling arena.

## DESTINY

**Destiny** is lightweight polyester rainwear fabric from **Travis Textiles** made of textured microfiber for a soft, quiet feel and hand. The fineness of the microfibers and the tight fabric structure both contribute to the fabric's water resistant, yet breathable, performance without coatings or laminates. For shorts, jackets, rainwear and activewear.

## DRYLOFT®

This is a two-layer fabric designed by **W. L. Gore & Associates** specifically for high loft, insulated products such as "baffled" jackets, parkas and sleeping bags. **The Dryloft®** membrane bonded to appropriate nylon rip-stop or polyester shell fabrics protects the insulating materials from wind and water penetration while offering an extremely breathable system for the garments, preventing moisture from condensing on the inside of the fabric.

## DUREPEL®

Offered by **Burlington Performance Fabrics**, **DUREPEL®** is a durable (stands up to repeated home washings), water and stain-repellent finish suitable for protection against snow and light rain. The DUREPEL® finish is applied to several Burlington fabrics commonly used in outerwear shell fabric applications.

## DUREPEL 1000®

**Burlington Performance Fabrics** weatherproof shell fabric features a specially engineered, durable (stands up to multiple home launderings) micro-porous coating that provides protection from wind and water while remaining breathable. **Durepel 1000®** is designed to be ideal for shell fabric applications in performance outerwear for moderate climatic conditions.

# WATERPROOF AND WINDPROOF, BUT BREATHABLE

## ENTRANT GII®

The **Entrant GII®** collection high-end performance fabrics from **Toray** are all based upon a unique, proprietary coating technique that creates three special layers within the foam itself that makes the fabric system waterproof and breathable. There are two types of the **Entrant GII®** performance fabric coatings available in the collection: The type "C" provides more "breathability" by being somewhat more permeable for water vapor to penetrate for comfort (and a little less totally waterproof), while type "P" provides outstanding waterproof performance and a bit less breathability. (Everything is a trade off.) Either coating can be obtained on different nylon or polyester fashion-oriented shell fabrics. Mountaineering, skiing, snowboarding, trekking and biking all use these fabrics.

## EPICAL®

**Somitex Printers** present their top-of-the-line shell fabric featuring a waterproof, windproof and breathable coating called **Epical®**, that surpasses any other of their high performance shell fabric collections. Applied to a wide range of tough microfiber woven fabrics, the collection is offered in both nylon and polyester fibers. For protection and excellent breathable comfort in performance shell fabrics, consider **Epical®**.

## EXOSKIN™

**Enterprise Coatings** offers a family of specially formulated performance waterproof polyurethane coatings for the water sport apparel and accessory industry. Using a selection of woven, non-woven and knitted substrates (the fabrics that form a foundation for laminates or coatings), the **Exoskin™** fabrics shed water, are windproof, resist weathering and sun aging and have remarkable stretch and recovery. Plus they are very tough, hard wearing and abrasion resistant. Where there's water, there is Exoskin™ fabrics in surfing gear, surface and scuba diving, kayaking and sailing apparel.

## FILA TECH®

**Fila USA** offers a high performance, lighter weight shell fabric with excellent wind resistance, water resistance and breathability that's ideal for 'windwear', high impact aerobic activities and warmups. Made from very finely and tightly woven microfibers, the **Fila Tech®** fabric won't permit wind penetration and will keep out all but the heaviest rain without the application of other special coatings, films or finishes.

## GORE-TEX®

**W.L. Gore & Associates** created the best known, high performance, durably waterproof, breathable and windproof membrane technology. This is applied to a wide range of performance outerwear, footwear and accessories used in backpacking, camping, skiing, running, golf, hunting and many other active pursuits. The use of the **Gore-Tex®** trademark is dependent upon the licensed manufacturer designing the finished product to meet Gore's GUARANTEED TO KEEP YOU DRY® standards. Gore-Tex® fabric constructions include two layer, three layer, z-liner and LTD. 20 years old in 1996, Gore-Tex® fabric is the most commonly branded membrane technology for durably waterproof, windproof and breathable performance.

## GORE-TEX® IMMERSION® TECHNOLOGY

A specially designed three layer fabric that is durably waterproof for fishing waders and "drysuits". Consisting of the Gore-Tex® membrane bonded to DuPont's tough Cordura* nylon shell fabric and a non-wicking, knitted lining fabric. The fisherman stays dry and comfortable, thanks to the fabric's unique ability to breathe underwater.

## GORE-TEX® OCEAN TECHNOLOGY®

Especially designed by **W. L. Gore & Associates** for offshore and coastal sailing gear, **Gore-Tex® Ocean Technology®** fabrics consist of three fabric layers bonded together to form a durably waterproof, windproof and very breathable outer shell to protect the sailor from the elements. Using a tough nylon or polyester woven shell fabric bonded to the high strength Gore-Tex® breathable membrane and then to a knitted polyester lining fabric that readily wicks moisture, this fabric system is truly seaworthy, meeting Gore's GUARANTEED TO KEEP YOU DRY® standards.

## GORE WINDSTOPPER®

**W. L. Gore & Associates** addresses the problems of wind chill with their **Gore Windstopper®** fabric designed for outerwear and accessories. The fabric is durably windproof and very breathable. Ideal for golf jackets, hunting and shooting gear, backpacking, skiing, cycling and general outerwear, Gore Windstopper® fabric stops wind while keeping you com-

fortable through the special membrane bonded to fleece and lining fabrics. It is available in two or three layer constructions.

## H₂NO® PLUS

When the weather really hits, **Patagonia** is ready with two approaches for maintaining comfort, both of which are grouped as **H₂NO® Plus**. These fabrics should not be considered as fabrics, but rather environmental "systems" ready to be styled into one-piece high performance suits. One approach takes a bi-laminate shell fabric made from a tightly woven, microdenier nylon for a tight, tough, wind resistant outer face and bonds it to the special H₂NO® Plus water resistant/breathable coating. This fabric is designed for light rain, snowboarding, Alpine skiing, etc. The other approach is a tri-laminate fabric with a microfiber nylon shell, the H₂NO® Plus breathable/water and wind-resistant coating in the middle and a special nylon tricot knit on the inside. This is designed to eliminate the need for a separate lining being used in the garment construction that could wet-out or bind during extended use. The tri-laminate is used in full "bibs" and snowmobile suits, jackets and pants for mountaineering and cold weather mountain activities in heavy snow or for trekking in winter.

## H₂NO® STORM

A lightweight champion of performance outerwear fabrics, **Patagonia H₂NO®** collection. The first of the H₂NO® shell fabrics is Storm®, a three layer fabric system made up of a tough, lightweight, woven rip-stop shell fabric that resists abrasion, a middle barrier membrane from Gore® technologies that is waterproof but breathable, and a light weight nylon tricot inner fabric that is treated to transfer and disperse moisture. When used by itself with ordinary clothing underneath, a H₂NO® Storm jacket and pants would keep you comfortable in cold conditions, but when it is worn with the right performance underwear, innerwear and accessories, the most severe mountaineering, skiing and wet conditions should be no problem.

## H₂OFF®

Not all waterproof/breathable fabrics need special coatings, treatments, membranes, etc. **Toray** presents its "Water Shed Architecture" approach in its **H₂Off®** fabric collection. The company has created a special microfiber polyester that looks and feels like a natural fiber and have wo-

WATERPROOF AND WINDPROOF, BUT BREATHABLE

# WATERPROOF AND WINDPROOF, BUT BREATHABLE

ven it into a particularly fine, tight and dense, super waterproof fabric structure. While even driving rain and wind are kept from entering the fabric, there are enough tiny spaces in the yarn and fabric structure to allow water vapor to escape and keep the fabric quite breathable. With a soft, supple hand, these fabrics comfortably protect for tennis, golf, skiing and hiking.

## HELLY-TECH® CLASSIC

**Helly-Tech® Classic** is a special bi-component coating that is waterproof yet has "the highest levels of moisture transportation", thanks to having a content of a combination of 85% micro-porous and 15% of **Helly-Hansen's** special hydrophilic (water loving) coating. Clothes made from fabrics treated with this coating are designed to be very comfortable and stay dry, even in the wettest conditions with the strongest exertion. Look for it in clothes for skiing, hiking, biking, fishing, camping and other action-oriented wear.

## HELLY-TECH® LIGHTNING

**Helly-Hansen** offers this lightweight, waterproof, yet breathable (offers a high level of moisture vapor transmission), coated fabric featuring an interesting combination of 15% micro-porous coating combined with an 85% hydrophilic coating. According to the proprietor, **Helly-Tech® Lightning** is even comfortable in humid weather during activity. Outerwear for lighter exercise is where you are going to find this product.

## HELLY-TECH® PRO

This coating is especially designed for garments intended for extreme use where maximum protection from wind and weather is a requirement, not a luxury. Made of 50% micro-porous coating and 50% hydrophilic coating, both the thickness and the component makeup of the fabric coating are selected to do the toughest jobs thrown at it. According to the manufacturer, in all cases involving **Helly-Hansen's** bi-component coatings, when the temperature and the moisture content within the garment increases in relation to the conditions outside the garment, the coating works to equalize the difference by moving more and more moisture. The greater the difference, the more effectively the coating works to transport moisture out of the garment. When activity decreases, the process reverses itself in the direct proportion to the slowing of activity and moisture production.

## HYDROFLEX®

A special coating that **Consoltex** in Canada puts on their **Hydroflex®** shell fabric makes the fabric waterproof as well as windproof, yet its coating structure allows water vapor to "breathe" through the fabric structure and through the coating to escape. This prevents the water vapor generated from the body to condense on the inside of the fabric and cause comfort problems with the wearer. When the Arctic winds howl north or south of the border, this performance outerwear fabric performs.

## HYDROTHANE®

**HydroThane®** from **National Dyeworks** is an environmentally friendly, water-based urethane coating for nylon, polyester and cotton woven fabrics destined for shell applications in jackets, outdoor apparel and accessories. The coating imparts water resistance to the fabrics, yet allows them to "breathe". In addition, the coating adds additional abrasion resistance to shell fabrics for outerwear.

## HYDRO VINYL®

**National Dyeworks** offers this breathable, but water resistant, water-based, environmentally friendly vinyl coating for nylon, polyester or cotton shell fabrics for jackets, coats and accessories. The coating is entirely solvent-free, yet is reputed to perform as well as solvent-based coatings and is said to increase abrasion resistance in the fabrics.

## K - KOTE®

**Kenyon Industries** has created a waterproof, windproof and breathable shell fabric coating using a special modified polyurethane coating material designed for rainwear and outerwear for hunting, backpacking, sailing wetwear and skiwear. They also offer a heavier weight, super-durable coating, called **K- Kote® Plus** for when the going really gets tough.

## KLAY - KOTE®

You say you are looking for waterproof and windproof shell fabrics? You say you want them to be easy care and durable? Look no further! **Kenyon Industries** has just the coating for you. Called **Klay Kote®**, it is a special pre-colored, urethane coating that looks good, keeps you water and windproof and is friendly to the touch. Rainwear, outerwear and "wetwear" for sailing are the places you can find this one.

## MARMOT MEMBRAIN®

**Marmot's Membrain®** is a waterproof - breathable fabric laminate

# WATERPROOF AND WINDPROOF, BUT BREATHABLE

featuring an excellent "monolithic" polyurethane shape-changing polymer layer that increases or decreases its vapor transfer capabilities depending upon the degree of generated heat by the body. The higher the activity, the warmer the body becomes and, likewise, the breathability of the laminate. When activity and heat production decreases, the laminate polymers return to their original shape and breathability decreases. Because it is monolithic (it has no holes in it), the laminate remains water and windproof under all conditions. Marmot calls it a "smart fabric" because of its ability to adjust to conditions and degrees of activity for maximum comfort for the wearer. Membrain® is ideal for a broad range of shell fabric for seam-taped, waterproof or insulated garments.

## MICROFT CONDENIER®

If you seek a super lightweight shell fabric that is waterproof, windproof, yet breathable, **Teijin America's Microft Condenier®** featherweight microdenier polyester fabric could fill the bill. Specially woven with a very high density woven structure (over 200 picks per inch) with very fine micro yarns, this fabric will not allow wind or water to penetrate, but water vapor can easily escape for breathable comfort - and the fabric does it without coatings, membranes or DWR finishes. It makes a great windbreaker weight pullover or jacket for golf, boating, jogging or even as a shell fabric for quilting or lamination with an insulating material for skiing, hiking, etc.

## P.E.F.®

Touted as the market's "warmest windproof fleece", this three-layer composite fleece fabric incorporates a special windproof/breathable membrane barrier (described as a "**P**erformance **E**nhancing **F**ilm") located between the outer shell fabric and the lining fabric. The shell fabric is an insulating and quick drying polyester fleece pile fabric (made of P.C.R.® recycled polyester) and the lining fabric is the "silk weight" Capilene® laminate fabric that is treated to quickly wick moisture away from the body and has a smooth surface that allows other layers in contact with it to slide without bunching up or sticking. This warm system can be found in **Patagonia's** pullovers, jackets, gloves and other accessories.

## PERMIA®

With wind and waterproof protection, yet with breathable comfort built-in (thanks to a special polyurethane coating developed in Japan),

# WATERPROOF AND WINDPROOF, BUT BREATHABLE

**Somitex Printers** offers a whole family of performance shell fabrics under the **Permia®** trademark. Available in a broad range of robust shell fabics made of polyester and nylon, they are all tough and ready to be environmentally challenged. These are bad weather friends and found in performance outerwear.

## PNEUMATIC®

Described as an endurance shell fabric for high exertion pursuits, **Patagonia's Pneumatic®** fabric bonds a lightweight polyester rip-stop shell fabric that has been treated with a durable water repellent (DWR) finish with an inner layer fabric that has a windproof, highly breathable pneumatic barrier that is water resistant. This is a formula for a high performance fabric designed with little weight, great flexibility with a lot of protection built-in. It is used in jackets and pants for running in poor conditions, mountain biking, cross country skiing, mountain biking and track skiing.

## POLARTEC® WINDBLOC®

**Malden Mills** offers a medium weight tri-laminate fabric system for outer shell applications designed to offer optimum protection from the weather. The **Polartec® Windbloc®** system is made up of three layers of performance materials that are permanently bonded together to offer superior windproofness and breathability (thanks to a permeable non-porous membrane that allows no wind in but allows body moisture vapor to escape). It has excellent warmth retention and moisture management (courtesy of a durable, comfortable, wickable inner pile fabric layer) and a durable, yet supple, wind resistant face. To be found in general outerwear and performance winter actionwear.

## PROOF ACE®

Whether it is a heavy downpour, wind-driven rain or a heavy sea, **Unitika America's Proof Ace®** shell fabric is reputed to handle the job and keep you dry and comfortable as well. Featuring a special high-tech micro-ceramic coating that keeps water out and, at the same time, allows moisture vapor to escape (breathable), it keeps the wearer dry both ways. For mountaineering or other abrasive outdoor sports or for foul weather gear for boating in gale conditions or on a foggy day, **Proof Ace®** could be your choice.

## SCHOELLER®- skifans

To keep warm and dry - and looking good - on the ski slopes is the challenge of the new **Schoeller®-**

# WATERPROOF AND WINDPROOF, BUT BREATHABLE

**"skifans"** stretch fabric for skiwear, snowboarding clothes. A stretch woven fabric (thanks to Lycra® spandex being built-in), the fabric offers the combination of high performance synthetic fibers and natural fibers to achieve its purpose. With a tough outer shell of polyamide (nylon), impregnated with special finishes that make it water and soil repellent, the inside of the fabric is a lightly brushed blend of very fine acrylic staple fibers and wool for cozy insulation and wonderful moisture management.

## SCHOELLER®- stretchlite

This hard exercise (expedition - class) stretch woven fabric design offers tough, but lightweight, performance with excellent weather resistant qualities and breathable comfort. **Schoeller®- stretchlite** combines Lycra® spandex for stretch, a brushed microdenier polyester and cotton layer next to the skin for comfort, warmth and moisture transmission, and a tough, impregnated polyamide skin for water and weather resistance. This makes a great fabric for stretch pants for skiing and backpacking as well as jackets, bibs and stretch bottoms.

## SCHOELLER®- WB-formula

Create a fabric with water and windproofness for a loose-fitting garment design with breathable comfort was the challenge and **"WB-formula"** and **"WB-formula Extreme"** fabrics were **Schoeller®'s** answer. They created stretch woven fabrics using Lycra® spandex (two-way and four-way) woven with special surface textures and then they combined them with an elastic, permeable membrane offering waterproof and windproof performance and good breathable properties. An ideal fabric for shell tops or bottoms, the **"WB-formula"** fabrics are lightweight and easily packable, and are a definite choice for cross country, trekking, biking, skiing, snowboarding or mountaineering styled into pants, jackets, suits and bibs. (**"WB-formula Extreme"** fabrics feature DuPont's Cordura® fibers on the fabric face for extra strength and abrasion resistance plus all the other bells and whistles.)

## SCHOELLER®- WB-400

This one is an "all-in-one" stretch woven fabric for winter sports and athleisure lounging offering all-weather comfort and performance in

# WATERPROOF AND WINDPROOF, BUT BREATHABLE

even the most extreme conditions or in the lodge. With a fully brushed insulating inner face made from high filament polyester with a wicking finish for moisture management and Lycra® spandex for stretch comfort, the **"WB-400"** fabric has an impregnated polyamide outer face to repel water and weather while allowing moisture vapor to escape for breathable comfort. **Schoeller's "WB-400"** fabric system can be found in top-of-the-line stretch pants for ski, riding clothes, backpacking gear, jackets and full active suits.

## SKIN FIT

**Skin Fit** is an extremely lightweight competitive swimwear fabric from **LaLame** that is a very fine woven two-way stretch fabric constructed from special fine denier yarns and Lycra® spandex, coated with 3M Scotchgard® for water and wind resistance. It offers superior lower coefficient of friction and lower drag in the water for the serious competitor, but is also great for cycling and for just spending the day at the beach looking and feeling good, wet or dry.

## STORMBREAKER®

If you are at sea about what kind of stormgear or dry suit fabrics you should consider for your next America's Cup race, perhaps you will want to look into **Helly-Hansen's** extensive **Stormbreaker®** collection. These foul-weather shell fabrics are variously coated, treated and bonded with water and windproof materials to make them stand up to nearly anything Mother Nature wants to throw at you. From competition dinghy suits to full "so'westers", this collection will keep your powder (and everything else) dry!

## STORM F.I.T.®

In creating the **Storm F.I.T.®** fabric, **Nike, Inc.** joined hands with W. L. Gore & Assoc. in combining a variety of fabrics, including an ultra-fine woven, microfiber polyester shell fabric (designed to repel water and wind), and an impervious membrane that gives the wearer water and wind protection, as well as maximum breathability. Nike's Storm F.I.T.® garments are all "seam sealed" to assure total water resistance. For maximum "all weather" protection, Storm F.I.T.® is ideal alone or in combination with Therma F.I.T.® or Dri F.I.T.® fabric systems, depending on the weather you find yourself in when you are hiking, running, snowboarding, backpacking, skiing or mountain biking.

# WATERPROOF AND WINDPROOF, BUT BREATHABLE

## STORM-TECH®

**Storm-Tech®** is a bi-laminate shell fabric from **Brookwood Company**. Special Taslan® nylon is tightly woven into a durable fabric, then is laminated to a "monolithic" (single-layer, non-porous) but breathable membrane that keeps out wind and wind-driven rain while allowing perspiration in the form of moisture vapor to escape. This provides longer lasting comfort and superior dryness for the wearer. The Taslan® (air-jet textured) face to the fabric gives it a friendly hand and the special membrane gives Storm-Tech® a friendly and dry comfort zone.

## SUPER MICROFT®

**Super Microft®** is **Teijin America's** trademark covering a broad range (10 to 15 different fabrics) of high performance shell fabrics for outerwear that have microdenier fibers, wind resistance and water resistance as their common performance basis. In some cases, the fabrics are made of nylon taffeta, in others, they are special polyester microfiber constructions. Some have **DWR** finishes (**D**urably **W**ater **R**esistant) while others have special coatings. Some feature high breathability while others claim to be totally waterproof; some offer moisture management and others insula-

tion. The Super Microft® collection is a good place to shop for high performance shell fabrics for outerwear and activewear.

## SYMPATEX®

This non-porous, ultra-thin membrane from **Akzo Nobel** is windproof, waterproof and breathable, offers insulating properties and can be permanently laminated to almost any textile. However, before you can apply the **Sympatex®** trademark to the product, you must be licensed to apply the trademark, meet the company's garment "make" standards by sealing all seams and test the laminated fabrics extensively to check the quality of the lamination. Outerwear, footwear, knitwear, hats, gloves, etc. are all protected by the Sympatex® mark and the high performance membrane technology it represents.

## SYMPATEX WINDLINER®

According to **Akzo Nobel**, **Sympatex Windliner®** is a totally nonporous membrane laminate that is absolutely windproof, water resistant, yet breathable. It is on an eco-friendly polyester film designed to be laminated with all sorts of knitted fabrics and is created for garments where lightweight flexibility is especially needed. Ideal for golfwear,

sweaters, fleeces and other sports-related and activewear apparel where total waterproofness is not required.

## TORAYDELFY 2000

Here is a fabric that was "born" for snowboarding. **Toray** made this lightweight, finely woven nylon shell fabric (sometimes polyester fibers are used) with an impervious, water repellent and wind resistant coating that still breathes even during the most active, stressful periods on the slopes yet still keeps water out. Also, this fabric could be described as "the quiet one" because it is noiseless. This one works as well in other activewear.

## TRIAD®

**Harrison Technologies, Inc.** has created a special laminate using DuPont's special Hytrel® polyester elastomer that exhibits strong moisture transmission properties while keeping rain and wind out. This film is enhanced by a new lamination process, called Capillact®, that pulls water vapor toward the Hytrel® layer for maximum efficiency in moisture management. Called **TRIAD®**, it is a high-performance, waterproof, windproof, breathable film laminate fabric with superior toughness, resilience, and overall superior performance in cold conditions or in higher temperatures. This laminate is ideal for high-performance shell fabrics for outerwear.

## TRIPHIBIAN®

This fabric is claimed to be the "ultimate fabric in technical fall/winter training". A knitted and bonded tri-laminate (three layers) from **InSport International**, **Triphibian®** combines two nylon layers with the Vapex® all weather, waterproof and breathable laminate layer in the middle. The inside nylon fabric layer next to the skin contains the Intera® moisture management process for efficiently wicking moisture away from the body and the outer fabric is a tightly knitted nylon and Lycra® spandex combination for wind and water resistance, compressive support and give-and-go comfort. Great for cycling and running tights, mountain biking and wet weather workouts.

## TRIPLE POINT CERAMIC®

**Lowe Alpine Systems** has created a high-performance shell fabric system that combines a special fabric structure with its unique proprietary coating and finish. This finish combines microporous polyurethane film with a coating of ultra-fine silicone micro-beads. The result is a durably waterproof, very breathable and

# WATERPROOF AND WINDPROOF, BUT BREATHABLE

wear-resistant fabric system that provides superior rain protection and breathable comfort for the wearer. **Triple Point Ceramic®** is available in a wide range of shell fabric applications in performance outdoor apparel.

## ULTRA MANIAC®

This lightweight, tough rip-stop woven fabric from **InSport** is quite a compact performance fabric package. It is actually a very complex, comprehensive combination of multiple features all rolled into one. First, it is woven from nylon microfiber yarns that offer excellent coverage, softness, water and wind resistance in a tear-resistant rip-stop construction. The outer surface of the fabric has an ultra-thin hydrophobic (water hating) coating, making it wind and waterproof, yet breathable. This is bonded on the inner surface of the fabric with a hydrophilic (water loving) film that transfers moisture from the skin and is claimed to prevent "loss of performance due to contact with body oils, salt and sweat". Add to this a 360° reflective printed surface that makes you shine at night when light hits you and you can safely jog, walk, run, bike or do any outdoor recreational activity day or night in all weather conditions.

## ULTREX®

**Burlington Performance Fabric's** top-of-the-line performance shell fabric system claims a perfect balance of protection and comfort in extreme climate conditions. Made up of fine, densely woven fibers, permanently bonded to a specifically engineered microporous coating that allows perspiration vapor to escape while keeping wind and water out, the **ULTREX®** fabric is then treated with Burlington's DUREPEL® durable, super water-repellent finish to complete the performance fabric system. Available for skiwear, snowboarding, golf and performance outerwear.

## VAPEX™

This is a specially formulated, high precision monolithic waterproof, but breathable, membrane of water-loving polyurethane that is custom-formulated and applied to a wide range of fabrics by **Enterprise Coatings Co., Inc.** The coating is cast on a variety of nylon and polyester knitted, woven and non-woven substrate fabrics that are sometimes napped or face finished, and they act as an outer barrier or as a functional barrier between two or more layers of fabric. The durable membrane offers high moisture vapor transmission

(breathability), high water resistance and windproofness as well as a superior hand, drape and stretch. Because Enterprise creates and casts the film in house on their own specially prepared substrate fabrics, they claim to have a greater quality control than other companies that only apply the critical membranes to someone else's fabrics.

## VERSATECH®

Another of **Burlington Performance Fabric's** special high performance shell fabric systems, **VERSATECH®** features special microfiber yarns, tightly woven into a dense weave and treated with Burlington's DUREPEL® super water-repellent finish offering a fabric with high water resistance, a soft, pliable hand, breathability and wind-proofness. Great for biking jackets, wind shirts and lighter weight outerwear.

## WHIRL WIND™

**Consoltex** has given this fabric an appropriate name, considering it is very wind resistant as well as repelling nearly any amount of water thrown at it or poured on it. Made of super fine, microfiber polyester yarns very tightly woven into both the warp and filling of the fabric, the resulting fabric needs no special coatings, films or membranes to keep the weather out while allowing water vapor to breathe out of the fabric for cold weather comfort or any exertion on a chilly, windy day. You'll find **Whirl Wind™** tags on some great golf jackets, cycling gear, hiking clothes and even outside of insulated skiwear.

## WINDBRAKE®

**Harrison Technologies, Inc.** presents **Windbrake®**, a tri-laminate fabric process (3 layers bonded together) using DuPont's special Hytrel® polyester elastomer to assure maximum moisture management and windproof performance for lighter duty fabrics. Brushed circular knit sweatshirt fabrics, napped tricot fabrics, wovens or other fabric combinations can be laminated using this technology to carry the Windbrake® trademark.

WATERPROOF AND WINDPROOF, BUT BREATHABLE

# STRETCH

In the old days of football, exceptional offensive players were called "triple threat men" (they could run the ball, pass it and kick it, and all with great skill). Today, with the advent of the "specialist" player, such athletes will probably never have a chance to show their talents in all three skills in the same game. Pity.

However, we do have a triple threat <u>product</u> that is scoring BIG in the performance apparel business and nearly everywhere in the sportswear and apparel markets. It is called STRETCH and it is a clean winner in <u>comfort, fit and performance</u> across a broad range of performance wear, team sports and almost every category of athletic, exercise and "street" apparel.

# STRETCH
## ADDING COMFORT, FIT AND
## SPECIAL PERFORMANCE TO ACTIVEWEAR

The art of incorporating stretch to fabrics varies widely, from adding a degree of flexibility to rigid fabrics, adding support or shaping the body, or forcibly containing the movement of selected muscle groups during exercise to improve and extend performance levels during exercise or competition. **To be considered as a "stretch" product, the material or fabric must have immediate recover nearly or totally to its original shape after "stretching".**

The materials and approaches to stretch can be summarized as follows:

### ▪ Bias Stretch:

The technique of cutting a rigid woven fabric diagonally at a 45° angle so it can be expected to stretch in a lengthwise direction in response to gravity's pull and move back to its original shape when pulled in a crosswise direction (a "scissoring" action).

### ▪ Natural Rubber or Latex:

The processed sap of the rubber tree that is processed and extruded into rubber fibers which are usually covered with other yarns to protect them from things that could weaken the rubber if in direct contact. Commonly used in waistbands, hosiery elastic, medical and athletic support bandages and wrappings and in some foundation fabrics.

### ▪ Spandex:

Introduced in 1959 by DuPont, spandex fibers are the most commonly used elastomeric (stretch) fibers in use. A melt spun continuous filament synthetic fiber, spandex is made in a wide range of weights (deniers) suitable for the most powerful fabrics used in compression fabrics and foundation fabrics as well as the lightest weight sheer mesh fabrics, stretch lace and women's sheer stockings and just about everything in between. Spandex is the generic (basic) name for this whole classification of synthetic stretch fibers.

### ▪ Textured Stretch Fibers:

Textured continuous filament fibers may be used to create stretch characteristics in woven or knitted fabrics.

### ▪ Stretch Films and Coatings:

A new classification of stretch materials growing out of the "waterproof, windproof and breathable" coatings.

The listed fibers or coatings that add the stretch feature to fabrics represent a relatively small percentage of the total fabric content, yet they create the "magic" necessary to add the comfort, drape, fit or performance we want in activewear and everyday wear.

# STRETCH
# COMFORT - FIT - PERFORMANCE

Real stretch in apparel is a relatively new development. Originally, there were only two ways you could achieve "stretch" in a woven fabric. One way would be to cut the fabric "on the bias" or diagonally to the "warp - filling" weave grid of a basic woven construction (this allowed the two sets of yarn, warp and filling, to move or "scissor" against each other, giving some stretch-like movement in an otherwise rigid structure). The other way was to use a silk fiber (continuous filament) with a very high twist in either the warp or filling (usually the filling) of a woven fabric. The fiber would act like a "spring" and allow the fabric to move a little in one direction or the other. This principle was also used in the "welts" or tops of ladies' stockings (before panty hose, of course).

The next step in stretch was the invention of knitted fabrics. Knitted structures – especially rib knits and jersey fabrics – have a good two-way stretch characteristic (mostly in the direction of width and, to a lesser degree, of length) that provides comfort to the wearer. However, these products provided little or no "power" recovery or control without some sort of "stretch" fiber being knitted in.

Although Charles Goodyear discovered how to vulcanize natural rubber in 1893, it wasn't until 1920 that U.S. Rubber invented fibrous rubber or "latex" yarns, which were generally used as a "core" fiber covered with another yarn or yarns. Even today, much of the latex rubber that is used is covered (uncovered latex is hard to dye and tends to harden in sunlight). However, with improvements in its durability and chemical resistance, latex rubber is still in great demand, especially for power bandages, waistbands and control panels in support underwear and foundations. Latex rubber has an elongation (stretch) of 700% to 900% with 100% recovery.

The next phase of "stretch" evolved from DuPont's research and development of continuous filament synthetic fibers, especially nylon or polyamide in the 1940's and after WWII. Nylon, like all succeeding continuous filament, petroleum-based fibers, is "thermosettable" or able to be softened by heat, shaped into another form and cooled, retaining its new shape from that point on. (In the case of nylon, this can be done only once in its 'life', but polyester can be reshaped at higher and higher heat levels several times until it finally melts or crystallizes.) This characteris-

# STRETCH
# COMFORT - FIT - PERFORMANCE

tic was quickly exploited in the late 1950's, 60's and 70's with various mechanical methods of thermosetting being used to twist, bulk and texture these fibers using heat and special mechanical processes. These texturing methods accomplished several purposes: adding bulk to the yarn – fluffing the fibers by putting tiny crimps in the filaments making up the fiber bundles/yarns; adding texture (irregular crepe or bouclé) to the finished knitted or woven fabric; and/or adding stretch, by setting a coiled, spring-like profile in the fibers that allowed the finished fabric to stretch and bounce back.

In fact, yarns having as much elongation as 400% (with good recovery) can be achieved with texturing techniques without the use of any true elastic (rubber or spandex) fibers. Such fibers are used for stretch hosiery, tights, leotards, swimwear, aerobicwear and other body-hugging clothing. In fact, a whole classification of comfort stretch, bottom weights woven fabrics (denims, chinos, etc.) with 50% elongation or more are now available in our market. Stretch polyester yarns are available in knitted fabrics with special performance stretch characteristics for other apparel applications.

The real "Stretch Revolution" had to wait until 1958-59, when DuPont introduced spandex fibers to the marketplace. Spandex was initially offered as a polyester-based product which was available in heavier denier weights to compete with latex in the support hosiery business, and in foundation garments, sock tops, some swimwear, waistbands, etc. In the 1980's, stretch began its strong move into the fabric manufacturing "mainstream" when polyether spandex fibers introduced by DuPont allowed finer spandex fibers to be created with better quality and uniformity.....and we never looked back!

# STRETCH
# COMFORT - FIT - PERFORMANCE

There are basically three major performance functions for stretch in the performance apparel-oriented products in this book:

## Comfort:

That wonderful, free feeling of having your clothes "give" with you when you move, especially when you find yourself in some pretty strange positions exercising, climbing, diving, running, biking, trekking or tackling.

## Fit:

Stretch is the key to form-fitting garments designed for exercise. Whether in luge or bobsled uniforms or in a competition swimsuit, close fit not only looks good, it can actually take fractions off your time that can mean all the difference. Also, most wicking moisture management systems are most efficient when they are in direct contact with the body, picking up the moisture to transport it for evaporation. Otherwise, it can "bead" and "puddle" on your skin.

## Performance:

Over the past several years, a whole new classification of stretch garments evolved, specifically designed to enhance performance in serious repetitious exercise or activity. These fabrics contain high percentages of heavier denier spandex with strong modulus (recovery) built-in. They are called "Com-

pression Fabrics" and they are designed to help control the athlete's major muscle "bundles" from over-flexing and moving around too much, wasting energy during strenuous activities. In fact, according to DuPont-sponsored research, a player's performance can be improved by as much as 12% wearing properly designed clothing made with Lycra® spandex. Compression is becoming a hot topic among real competitive athletes and even with people who take their exercise seriously.

Related to "power" stretch fabrics in this category are all of those specialized fabrics designed to support various body areas of an athlete, or active participant: (a) to prevent injury; (b) to help contain and/or to help heal an injury; (c) help control unwanted body movement (i.e., sports bras, etc.), (d) help shape the body as desired (foundation-type garments). These functions are served by a wide variety of elastic fabrics available in all sorts of modulus (recovery power) characteristics, fabric widths, types of elastic fiber coverings, and special fabric designs specially engineered for specific purposes from wide fabric form down to elastic tapes.

Today we have a new entry into the world of stretch. Its predecessor was probably some material like sheet foam latex that is commonly used for scuba suits, surfing gear and some snowwear.

# STRETCH
# COMFORT - FIT - PERFORMANCE

This new category is a classification of ultra-fine stretchable, permeable membranes that are used to bond two or more fabrics together and add waterproof, windproof and breathable properties to the composite fabric systems. These new materials allow the entire bonded system to have good, but limited, four-way stretch flexibility and comfort without delamination from the bonded fabric(s). Watch this development for further growth in the future.

**In the following section we will list products that offer stretch as a primary performance feature as well as products that have stretch as a value-added function.** If the primary function of the product is not stretch, we will give you only the product name and the section category in which you can find a full description. The products that feature stretch as their primary feature will be described in full, as in the other sections. Now, let's "extend" ourselves and visit the world of stretch and its uses.

STRETCH

# STRETCH
# COMFORT - FIT - PERFORMANCE

## COMPREXX®

Five years ago, **Darlington Fabrics** created one of the original "compression" fabrics and had it field tested and laboratory certified as having a direct, positive effect on improving athletic performance. This work on the **Comprexx®** fabric collection gave birth to the whole concept of compression fabrics for all sorts of athletic and team sports where repetitive actions can cause muscle fatigue unless the muscles are contained and controlled. Also certified under the DuPont Lycra® Power program for compression fabrics, these fabrics prevent the major muscle bundles from "over flexing" and moving around too much, wasting energy in strenuous activities. The fabrics are made of various fibers combined with heavier denier Lycra® spandex for higher power ("modulus") needed to do the job.

## DARLEXX SUPERSKIN®

When "fast" has to be "FASTER" in competitive sports, all things being equal, you may need an "edge". That's where **Darlington's Darlexx Superskin®** fabric could help. One of Darlington's Darlexx® collection of omni-directional stretch fabrics with all of the other performance perimeters built-in, this fabric has a urethane film bonded to the fabric face that is ultra-smooth, reducing drag in air or water. Combine that with the fabric's snug, form fit and elasticity and you have the slickest game in town! Whether down the luge course, on the "expert" ski slope or in the pool, Superskin® could be "the edge" you were looking for.

## DARLEXX®
## THERMALASTIC®

There is a real performance alternative to neoprene in skiwear or warm water diving gear. **Darlington Fabrics Corporation** has created a wonderful fabric system starting with a warp knitted fabric (having little bulk or weight) that is brushed on the inside for insulation and then bonded with Darlington's special thermoplastic, four-way stretchable membrane that is waterproof, yet breathable, and windproof. This is combined with a tough, abrasion-resistant outer shell fabric made of a combination of polyester and Lycra® spandex treated with DuPont's Teflon® DWR water resistant finish. Ready for the slopes or the reefs, you'll find ski jackets and pants and warm water wet suits carrying the tags.

## E.C.T.®

**E.C.T.®** (**E**ngineered **C**omfort **T**echnology) is **Liberty Fabric's** trademark umbrella for a group of compression fabrics for serious exercise compression garments (shorts, tights, bodysuits, upper body garments, etc.) that have been tested and certified

# STRETCH
# COMFORT - FIT - PERFORMANCE

under the DuPont Lycra® Power fabric program. These fabrics offer the athlete enhanced performance and reduction of fatigue in strenuous, repetitive exercise by helping to control the unwanted movement of muscle bundles during impact exercise and repeated flexing. (In addition, it is claimed that compression fabrics can actually "train" the muscle groups to anticipate a specific exercise or motion and reduce the amount of energy necessary to start all over again in creating a desired motion every time it is desired. This has been named "proprioception".) These fabrics are treated for enhanced moisture management and have been specially engineered for specific sporting activities, and to insure comfort to the athlete.

## ESP®

If "affordable comfort stretch" is desired in a woven or knitted fabric, it is possible that **Trevira's ESP®** (**E**xtra **S**tretch **P**erformance) textured filament polyester will fill the bill. Created from a special polymer, this polyester fiber is specially textured with a high degree of crimp that allows the yarn to have a relatively high degree of elasticity and recovery. (This is a very different approach to stretch and elasticity than spandex, which has greatly more elasticity and stretch and has a much stronger "modulus" or recovery power.) ESP® is commonly used as a filling yarn in woven fabrics such as denim, providing one-way comfort stretch and recovery or is used in knitted fabrics to produce two-way stretch. It can be found in a broad range of active apparel ranging from swimwear to jeans, cycling wear, tights fashion, and other bottom weights.

## FITNESS SLIMMERS®

"Aerobics and exercise never felt better!" says **Danskin**, thanks to their special power net construction for shapewear featuring DuPont's Supplex® and Lycra®. Designed for comfort, the **Fitness Slimmers®** group uses a power net fabric to control the stomach, thigh and derriere areas so you can look good while getting in shape. For added comfort, a CoolMax® gusset has been incorporated. Danskin's specially designed Sports Bras also feature CoolMax® linings that wick away unwanted moisture and are carefully constructed to reduce the inevitable "bounce" in exercise, because Danskin wants you to feel good and look good at the same time.

## MCT®

**Moving Comfort** offers this unique fabric made from a combination of 60% wickable polyester, 10% rayon for softness, warmth, absorbency and super bright colors, plus 8% Lycra®

spandex for support, stretch, recovery and comfort. Ideal for sports bras, running gear and the like, **MCT®** is for both cool as well as cold conditions.

## REPLAY®

A special intermediate weight nylon fiber provides the foundation for this actionwear fabric from **Liberty Fabrics** for cycling, running, climbing and water sports. Made with 16% Lycra® spandex in a tricot construction (for excellent two-way stretch and recovery), **Replay®** contains more robust denier-weight filaments in the nylon than in most nylon/Lycra constructions intended for these uses, resulting in increased durability and "bounce-back" in the fabric and excellent fit and strength.

## SPANDURA®

This is a collection of one-way or two-way stretch fabrics that are designed for strength and for applications where flexibility is required. **Spandura®**, from **H. Warshow & Sons, Inc.**, is made from a special woven or knitted combination of DuPont's tough Cordura® nylon and Lycra® spandex fibers. Together they form tough, abrasion-resistant fabrics that fit perfectly, yet move with you and maintain their shape fully. With a choice of one or two-way stretch, plus the choice of being laminated with a polyurethane film for waterproofness, Spandura® is ready for all sorts of challenging tasks in performance apparel, boots and accessories. Spandura® is also available with a Teflon® water resistant finish.

## SPANDURA® II

The lighter weight version of **Warshow's** Spandura® performance stretch fabric collection, the **Spandura® II** fabric group is comprised of knitted (circular knitted and warp knitted), two-way stretch fabrics made from a finer denier Cordura® nylon and Lycra® spandex from DuPont. They are ideal for body-hugging garments for biking, jogging, biking, running and a whole lot of other active clothing that must have long-wearing performance and athletic stretch and recovery.

## SPANDURA® FLEX-TEX™

**Warshow** presents a new variation on its Spandura® two-way stretch fabric technology designed for pants for rock climbing, rollerblading, mountain biking or any other activity that threatens to remove your hide and destroy your clothes. Rough and tough as a rock face, **Spandura® Flex-Tex™** combines super-tough Cordura® nylon and Lycra® spandex with the comfort and moisture management of a soft terry lining made of DuPont's Supplex® nylon. Need 'give', breathability, wind resistance, abrasion resistance and insulation? Think Flex-Tex™.

# STRETCH
# COMFORT - FIT - PERFORMANCE

## SUPERLOC®

**Liberty Fabrics** has patented this special warp knitted collection of compression fabrics that have a special way to fuse an extra amount of Lycra® spandex fibers into the fabric structure during the finishing process. This locks in the spandex fibers and gives two-way stretch to the fabrics. With high elongation and modulus (power recovery) to enhance the serious athlete's performance and stamina by controlling muscle movement in exercise, these fabrics are all tested and certified under DuPont's stringent Lycra® Power program requirements. **Superloc®** fabrics are available in compression shorts, competitive swimwear, fitness wear, tights, sports bras, etc.

## SYNSATION™

This broad fabric collection from **Dyersburg Corp.** is made from special high filament, yarn-dyed polyester (dyed in yarn form before being made into fabric, which gives improved colorfast performance) and Lycra® spandex yarns for extraordinary fit and comfort in swimwear, aerobics and other bodywear. The high filament fiber content is reputed to enhance the fabric's moisture management (wicking) performance, yet the fabric itself absorbs very little moisture because of the hydrophobic (water hating) character of the polyester fiber.

STRETCH

# SPECIAL PRODUCTS

## SPECIAL PRODUCTS
## OTHER MIRACLES

Now we have reached the section in our Dictionary where we can recognize the special products that dot the market to fill in the performance "spaces" that either have not been addressed by other products or have only been a secondary feature as opposed to a "primary" performance attribute. These products are diverse and cover topics of concern ranging from insect and snake protection to showing up in headlights at night while exercising outdoors.

# SPECIAL PRODUCTS
# OTHER MIRACLES

**Before we get into some of the special products we would like to address one segment of the performance apparel industry - the "Team Sport" industry. We have some team sport products in this section of our first edition of the Dictionary, but what is included cannot be described as comprehensive. We would appeal to and invite those manufacturers, designers and suppliers of Team Sport performance apparel products to submit their branded products to us for inclusion in our next edition. We promise to have a more complete listing of such products in the future.**

Let's examine some of the needs we haven't discussed before, as well as the approaches and solutions that are currently being offered.

**Anti-bacterial/Anti-microbial/ Anti-fungal Processes and Treatments:** One of the hottest "value added" features currently available in the performance business, these processes involve an anti-bacterial/ anti-microbial/anti-fungal chemical being added to or built into a fabric or fiber for the purpose of retarding and preventing the growth of bacteria, microbes or fungus. Growth of bacteria causes odors, mildew and fungus as well as deterioration and staining in fabrics and associated potential health problems, such as ath-

letes' foot, etc. "Anti-microbial" treatments are now being added to a wide variety of products as a performance "plus". In the case of some polypropylene yarns, the anti-microbial chemicals are permanently built into the fiber itself when it is made.

**Puncture-proof, Tearing and Abrasion Resistance:** There are a whole bunch of "tough customers" out there in the performance fabric world. Not only are they made of durable fibers like nylon and polyester built into rugged, tear-resistant constructions, like "rip-stop", some are even made from the toughest fibers known to man! These include aramid fibers, such as Kevlar®, Nomex® and Trevar® and Spectra® polyethelene, all of which are also used for bullet proof clothing and body armor. If that were not enough, there is one company that weaves in strands of STEEL for good measure! (The aramid and polyethelene fibers are already stronger than steel by weight.) Climbing a mountain covered with razor blades? No worry. Fall off your "bike" on a gravel road at 70 mph? You might not make it, but your clothes will! Talk about performance!

**Reflectivity:** More and more people are finding themselves exercising in all sorts of ways out-of-doors and after dark, especially in the winter months. More competitions and outings are being held on

129

SPECIAL PRODUCTS

62

the road at twilight or after dark (running, biking, etc.), making these activities more and more dangerous without some sort of approach to improve the visibility of the roadside athlete to the evening or nighttime driver. New and exciting products are now available that are more attractive, affordable and effective than ever before. These products not only light up your life, they can save it!

**Team Sport Fabrics:** As mentioned before, the world of team sport has fabrics and performance requirements and categories of product that seldom find their way into "mainstream" sporting goods apparel retailing. However, with the advent of the team-brand and "licensed" retail merchandising approaches being taken across the country, more and more of this type of "authentic" and replica merchandise is finding its way into the market to tempt the fan. Certainly, all of the performance concerns listed in the prior sections of the book are of vital interest to the team sport industry, from moisture management, to insulation, to WPB and beyond. However, here are some special team sport mesh and coordinating products that deserve special mention.

**Insect Repellency:** If you are sensitive to insects or concerned about insect-borne disease, we have a product listing that offers real protection with a carefully certified and tested insect repelling fabric. Then

you can really tell them crawly critters to "Bug off!"

**Snake-proof:** Check out the "snake-proof" fabric listed here. It should give you a feeling of confidence when you are trekking through the "bush" where our slinky friends live.

**Quiet Fabrics:** Someone once said that "silence is golden". If you are a hunter, this phrase has new meaning and there are products designed not to be seen or heard.

**Stain Resistant/Soil Release Finishes:** We have listed some famous durable finishes for fabrics that are designed to resist the penetration of any liquid-borne stain or to allow any oily stain or soil to be cleaned or washed out of the fabric with ease. These finishes are either built into synthetic fibers when they are created; are applied to synthetic, or natural fiber blended fabrics in dyeing and finishing, or are applied by spray after those processes are over and "cured" or driven into the fibers and fabric by heat and, sometimes, pressure. One finish is very resistant to moisture penetration and won't let moisture of any kind penetrate the fabric or the fibers. Another finish contributes to a fabric's absorbency or "wicking" character and allows moisture to easily penetrate and move through the fabric for evaporation. At the same time, it allows washing detergent to penetrate

the fabric structure to carry away soil and oil-borne stains. Either way, the treated fabrics look better and perform longer.

**"Speed" Finishes:** There are specific finishes that are specially designed to be ultra-smooth and "slick" when applied to other fabrics. In this case, the finish or film is applied to competitive swimwear, speed skating, biking, etc., fabrics containing spandex that not only hug the body, but are also VERY smooth, offering little or no drag in the water or the air during competition. The idea is to add fractions of a second to a competitor's lap time or race time. Competitive bike riders and other athletes who compete in events measured in milli-seconds should look into these products.

**"Spacer" Fabric:** Here is a new fabric construction concept that is designed to provide the athletic shoe with a new cushioned shoe lining that will never break down (like foam), but rather stays "springy" over the life of the shoe. It is a special knitted structure that creates two separate fabric faces made of nylon. The two layers are tied together with a heavier, stiffer nylon yarn, forming a "sandwich" fabric with two faces and a "pile" of yarn connecting these while keeping them apart. When this structure is placed in the bottom of a shoe or "sneaker", the connecting fiber acts like a spring or cushion when compressed. This cushioning

system will never break down or wear down and stays "springy" and "breathable" for the life of the shoe. Talk about fabric innovation for performance wear!

**Flame Retardance:** Although usually thought of as an important property of tents, sleeping bags and such, flame retardance can be an important feature in performance apparel as well. Either it is the property of the fiber itself (such as a flame resistant chemical built into the synthetic fiber when it is created) or it is added to the fabric after it is made. Generally, these materials are flame retardant, not fireproof. This means that they will resist burning or will not sustain burning, under most conditions.

These are just some of the major "miracle" products and processes we list in this section of our Dictionary. Be assured that they represent only a small cross section of all of the wonderful products that are out there ready to keep you safer or more comfortable, or, perhaps, to help you perform better or just to help you look good while you do what you're doing. Look for them when you shop or when you are seeking value-added features for your performance apparel selections. You can be sure there are many more such products on their way to you in the future.

# SPECIAL PRODUCTS

## AZUREAN™

Just when we thought it was safe to go out in the sun with our clothes off and with sun block on, **ICON, U.S.A.** informs us that we aren't even safe from the potentially dangerous UV rays even when we are wearing clothes out of doors! ICON's research have shown that ordinary T shirts only allow an equivalent sun block protection of about 6 (SPF 6). By treating knitted and woven natural fiber fabrics with their patented process, they are able to achieve an equivalent sun block protection (SPF) of 50+ wet or dry. The process is claimed not to change the aesthetics of the fabric and, as an added feature, their tests claim that you will feel 5 to 10 degrees cooler in **Azurean**™ fabrics. There is something new under the sun!

## COVILLE'S AUTHENTIC AM MICROSTOP™

**Coville, Inc.** offers a new generation of polypropylene fabrics that have a special anti-microbial chemical built into the fiber's polymer structure when the fiber is made. The yarns and fabrics are also available in great colors that are also built into the fibers during the extrusion process, making them washfast, fade-proof and unaffected by any conditions of wear or cleaning. The anti-microbial properties protect the wearer against odor-causing bacteria, mildew, odor or mold and the development of

fungus for the life of the garment. The knitted fabric collection containing **Coville's Authentic AM Microstop**™ is quite broad and can be found in all sorts of performance inner and outerwear.

## DAZZLE FABRIC®

**Ames Textiles/Game Time Dazzle Fabric®** is a solid, high luster, heavyweight tricot fabric that complements the mesh fabrics on the playing field. Its special construction assures comfort and fit with tough nylon yarns providing durability and abrasion resistance. The super-bright fabric face brings the vibrant team colors to life while colorfast dyeing keeps them looking that way wash after wash, game after game.

## DIAMONDBACK®

Originally designed for the soccer field, this specially designed diamond-shaped mesh fabric has found its way on to the American football field (and other fields) as well. This fabric "made the cut" by combining a great look with excellent breathability with heavy duty abrasion resistance. For a "Pro" look and performance in athletic shirts, **Diamondback®** Mesh from **Game Time Fabrics** is the source.

## DURAKNIT®

Not all performance fabrics are complex combinations of ultra-high tech materials. Many are the rock foundation of the business with tough, high performance strength and comfort built in. **Duraknit®** from **Yarrington Mills Corp.** is one of these. Knitted primarily from textured nylon yarns, the fabric is specially finished in a most relaxed manner possible in order to fully relax the textured fibers, eliminating any residual shrinkage in the cloth. The result is a tough, durable team uniform fabric with plenty of "give-and-go" and "tackle toughness". Coordinating trim is also available.

## EXPEL®

If insects or vector disease control are a concern in your active lifestyle, you will want to know about **Expel®** fabrics from **Graniteville Fabrics division of Avondale Mills**. The Permethrin in this line of treated fabrics repels mosquitoes, ticks, spiders and other flying and crawling insects. Expel® uses Permethrin, a synthesized compound that closely resembles botanical compounds that have insecticidal properties. Permethrin was registered by the EPA as required by law after extensive review of required information, including product chemistry, toxicology, environmental fate metabolism and performance data. Easy care and washable (not dry cleanable), it is available in hunting and fishing garments, coats, jackets, coveralls, vests, headbands, camping gear, etc. No sense in being "bugged" by the great outdoors.

## FILA 5

Here is a performance shell fabric from **Fila USA** for wind jackets and wind pants with a patent leather-like, ciré face that gives it a great fashion look as well as excellent wind resistance and water repellence without losing softness and flexibility. A special soft, bright, easy care coating makes it so. Who said that function had to look dull and practical?

## HYDROFLAME®

If flame protection is a concern in your outdoor apparel, you may want to consider **National Dyeworks' HydroFlame®** coated fabrics for outerwear applications. It is a water-based, flame retardant coating that can be applied to most nylon, polyester or cotton shell fabrics and is environmentally friendly, as opposed to similar coatings that are solvent-based in application. Fabrics coated with HydroFlame® meet highest flame retardant standards for apparel applications.

## illumiNITE®

Athletic activity does not stop when the sun goes down. In fact, in many cases, this is the only time many fitness devotees can get in their miles, kilometers or laps. To keep them safe, **reflective technologies, inc.** has developed a remarkable coating process to infuse millions of highly

reflective sataLITE DISH® reflectors into the fabrics, either over all or in printed patterns. These tiny concave "mirrors" reflect light back to the original light source, focusing and maximizing the silhouette form of the wearer to the motorist. This retro-flective effect is being called "The illumiNITE® Matrix". **illumiNITE®** is available in woven and stretch fabrics including Supplex® nylon and in microfibers offering moisture management, water resistance and wind resistance as well as safety illumination. Jackets, vests, shorts, caps, tee shirts and all sorts of apparel and accessories for the active life are all available to light up your life and, perhaps, save it.

## inSIGHT®

That early morning or late evening jog, walk or cycling routine of yours just became safer, thanks to **InSport** and their line of reflective printed fabrics, featuring the new illumiNITE® products from reflective technologies. They are getting "glowing" reviews from all those athletes who have to bend their training schedules to fit their life schedules. Applicable to all sorts of fabrics, the reflective prints do not affect any other performance characteristics of the fabrics. For 360° visibility in the dusk or dark, think **inSight®**.

## LYCRA® POWER

This is a **DuPont** trademark that is being licensed for use on garments that meet DuPont approved performance standards. Designed and engineered for the competitive and serious athlete, the power of "compressive control" built into fabric can make all the difference between achieving maximum performance in sport or just an exercise. Muscle fatigue is the enemy in athletic competition and the compressive control of power stretch fabric with **Lycra®** hugs the muscle bundles and prevents any unnecessary and unwanted muscle vibration or movement. According to test data, a player's performance can be improved by as much as 12% wearing properly designed compression clothing made with Lycra®. DuPont's Lycra® Power trademark certification program is designed to assure that the compression fabrics and garments carrying the name have been tested and certified to do this job properly. Don't use the name without their OK first.

## MICRO MESH®

**Ames Textiles/Game Time** makes a lot of team sports mesh fabrics and uniform fabrics. **Micro Mesh®** is one of their premier items. Made of either polyester or nylon with a fine mesh design for excellent breathability, this tricot fabric has comfort stretch without elastic fibers. The fabric is commonly used in athletic shirts, shorts and other team sports apparel.

## MICROSAFE® ACETATE

A special acetate fiber (acetate is a close relative to rayon protection) has been designed by **Celanese Acetate** to provide continuous, built-in control of the spread of bacteria, fungi, mold, mildew and yeast. Acetate is a very absorbent fiber with an open pore structure that allows easy migration of moisture and prints and dyes easily. **MicroSafe®** is usually combined with other fibers in underwear, socks and shoes where warm, damp conditions can invite bacterial growth and mildew.

## MICROTEP - 25®

For the competitive swimmer, milli-seconds are everything and any "edge" helps at the finish. **TYR Sport** has created a new generation of competitive swimwear fabrics that combine the lightweight softness of microfiber with the water resistance of DuPont's slick Teflon® finish. This combination reduces the traditional fabric's thickness and weight as well as allows the water to run past and run off smoothly. In addition, increased chlorine resistance is built-in with the fabric remaining breath-

able and looking GREAT. The "fast one" could be wearing **Microtep-25®** next time.

## NU BLEND®

**Russell Athletic** presents a unique combination of a special blend of low-pill polyester and combed cotton (50/50 blend), spun with a special, proprietary spinning system that reduces the "hairiness" of the resulting yarn. It is dyed in tubular form to achieve the maximum in a relaxed, tensionless dyeing that helps control shrinkage. The whole process yields a very low pilling family of fleece and jersey fabrics that are shrinkage controlled and continue to look great wash after wash. Look for **Nu Blend®** fabrics in all sorts of Russell warm-up and exercise outfits.

## PRO-BRITE®

If you need a mesh fabric that can stand up to professional punishment and look great, **Game Time Fabrics** may have the mesh for you. **Pro-Brite®** is a heavier, team weight, durable nylon mesh fabric with a wonderful bright luster that stands out and makes team colors look sharp and bright. It is a highly breathable mesh with excellent abrasion resistance, even at the bottom of a fumble pile. Not only is it used in team sport uniforms, it can be found in other activewear in the market as well.

# SPECIAL PRODUCTS

## REACT®

**Converse, Inc.** offers their special athletic shoe lining, **React®**, that provides excellent cushioning characteristics. This occurs through the use of a special encapsulated cushioning material that absorbs energy by moving relative to the position and extent of the load placed on it. This material does not break down, like foams and other types of cushioning materials commonly used in athletic shoes, no matter how many jump balls you have to win.

## RHINO® CLOTH

Rhinos are famous for tough hides and **Thomaston Mills' Rhino® Cloth** can share the same distinction for durability and abrasion resistance, thanks to the use of DuPont's Cordura® nylon fiber in a special woven fabric construction. Look for it in shoes, boots and packs. (Fortunately, **Rhino® Cloth** is a lot more user friendly than the real thing!)

## SATIN PRO MESH®

For stretchable comfort in a team sports mesh fabric, **Ames Textiles/ Game Time** has created the **Satin Pro Mesh®** fabric using special stretch nylon fibers in an engineered mesh construction. Not only that, the face fibers are the brightest to be found, giving this heavy duty beauty the shiniest surface of any mesh available. But this fabric has more than just a pretty face (and a soft hand) - it is also scrimmage tough and abrasion resistant. Team uniforms and actionwear is where you'll find this one.

## SCHOELLER®- dynatec

If you ride motorcycles and want to protect your hide, you may be interested in **Schoeller®- dynatec** fabric. It is specially designed to resist hard abrasion and tearing while protecting against wind penetration. Its toughness and comfort comes from a special woven construction and from the use of DuPont's tough Cordura® fiber that can take a beating and survive most falls. Also, it is available printed with highly reflective materials for night safety. You could use this fabric in mountain climbing and snowboarding or any other rough sport where serious falls could painfully remove various parts of your skin or pieces of your anatomy.

## SCHOELLER®- keprotec®

Motorcycle racing inspired the development of this ultra-tough, flexible fabric designed to provide the maximum protection of traditional leather apparel, while offering a high degree of comfort and freedom of movement. To achieve this performance in one fabric, **keprotec®** fabrics are constructed using a complex array of fibers and finishes to accomplish the task: Cordura® nylon adds strength and breathability; Kevlar® super-strength aramid fibers (used in bullet proof vests) add maximum strength and tear resistance (four times the strength of steel, by weight!); and special finishes add rain and water resistance and soil release for easy care. For bike clothing of all kinds, mountain gear, skiing clothes, trekking or snow boarding or even for patches in high wear areas, keprotec®.

## SCHOELLER®- keprotec® with Inox

Just when you thought it was tough enough with **Schoeller®'s keprotec®** fabric with the super toughness of Kevlar® aramid fibers built-in, along comes **keprotec® with Inox**. Before, you couldn't wear it out or tear it - now you can't cut it! Why? They added a steel-reinforced thread in the construction that prevents it. The fabric still does all the other great stuff that good old keprotec® does and the applications are the same. However, this fabric is designed specifically for those who hang around sharp rocks and really rough places, like hanging on to mountains, glaciers or bouncing off gravel-covered bike roads.

## SILENZZ®

A new shell fabric has been developed by **Glen Raven Mills** that has been especially designed to promote "silence" in the fabric application. If noise is a problem when your jacket rustles or "whispers" and gives you away when you move around in the wild, **Silenzz®** fabrics could be your choice. Made with special water and wind resistant characteristics built-in, thanks to the fabric's construction and special finishing processes, look for the "quiet one" in hunting and other outdoor outer apparel.

## SKIN FIT

**Skin Fit** is an extremely light weight competitive swim wear fabric from **LaLame** that is a very fine woven two-way stretch fabric constructed from special fine denier yarns and lycra® spandex, coated with 3-M scotchguard® for water and wind resistance. It offers a superior lower coefficient of friction and lower drag in the water for the serious competitor. It is also great for cycling or for just spending the day at the beach looking and feeling good wet or dry.

## SPECTRA®/SOLUTION 7

The ultra-tough shell/backpack rip-stop fabric from **Travis Textiles** made with Allied Signal's **SPECTRA/Solution 7** has super strong, high performance polyethylene and high tenacity, textured ANSO-TEX nylon in a tough rip-stop woven construction for ultimate strength and abrasion resistance.

# SPECIAL PRODUCTS

Mountain climbing, trekking and hard-trail backpacking gear and the packs that go with it carry the tags.

## STUNNER®

**Toray** offers no bells and whistles with this fabric - only comfort, fit and feel. **Stunner®** is a special, high-tech polymer fiber/fabric combination designed to look and feel like cotton, but with the performance and easy care of synthetics. No special tricks - just a beautiful woven synthetic fabric that feels good and looks good to wear. The perfect cover-up or top and shorts for the beach, hiking, tennis, golf or just for casual wear.

## STUNNER® QD

Take the Stunner® fabric from **Toray**, add wicking performance for increased comfort and you have **Stunner® QD** (**Q**uick **D**ry) . Fortunately, to get this performance plus, you don't have to give up any of the other aesthetic virtues of this fabric "family".

## TACKLE II™/ GUARDIAN™

This pair of tough fabrics comes to us from **Consoltex, Inc.**, Canada, where it can be a hard world, indeed, whether off shore on the Grand Banks in a gale or hanging off some icy crag in the Canadian Rockies. Made of tough nylon that is U.V. (ultraviolet light) resistant, this pair of rugged customers have passed the toughest strength and durability standards the government (theirs or ours) can throw at them. If you want your snowmobile suit or ocean-going wet gear to outlast almost anything, you might want to try this stuff.

## TEFLON®

It's not a bad idea to confuse this **Teflon®** performance fabric finish with a frying pan coating. Not only do they have a common parent, **DuPont**, this tough, invisible finish will prevent the eggs (or anything else, for that matter) from sticking to your clothes, just like the pans. This Teflon® is a special, durable fabric finish that can be applied to any textile requiring water and oil-based stain protection - and it does this without disturbing the other performance attributes of the fabric it is used on. With this finish applied, water and other liquids merely run off the fabric without penetration and staining. Even if you wash or dry clean the fabric, just like the pans, the finish just keeps on protecting your stuff.

## TIDAL WAVE®

**Consoltex Inc.** offers a tear-resistant, five-ply nylon woven fabric that looks great in spite of its tough reputation. It provides the foundation for a wide variety of finishes to be applied to the base cloth to add whatever performance parameters the customer might desire. This fabric is at home in the surf as well as on the slopes as a ski shell or for snowboarding. Even team sport jackets feature **Tidal Wave®** fabrics.

## TOUGHTEK®

If you need to get a grip on things, **Harrison Technologies, Inc.'s Toughtek®** may be your answer. It is a special chemically treated fabric collection designed to offer a very reliable grip in wet or dry conditions. Offering high durability, Toughtek® is commonly found in glove palms, shoulder straps, shoe soles and hand grips in sports gear.

## VIPER® CLOTH

Whether you are on safari or just backpacking or strolling in the great outdoors, you might feel safer if your boots are made from **Thomaston Mills'** snake-proof **Viper® Cloth**. Made with a special weave and with super-tough Cordura® nylon from Dupont, many a sneaky snake has dented a fang on this stuff and kept the wearer safe.

## VISA®

**Visa®** is one of those "pioneering" trademark programs that established the importance of a performance, value-added process to an ordinary product in the textile industry as a way to enhance the product's merchandising worth. **Milliken & Co.** developed a special wicking/soil-release finish for their polyester fibers and fabrics and branded the finished products Visa®, not as "polyester". Visa® is a trademark that appears on a very broad range of fabrics from Milliken for all sorts of end use products, including activewear, performance wear and sporting apparel. Aside from the basic moisture management wicking properties and their associated soil release properties (especially oil-borne stains and greasy dirt), some of the products carrying the Visa® ID are heat retentive and abrasion resistant as well.

# TRADEMARKS
# LISTED
# ALPHABETICALLY
# WITH
# PROPRIETORS

# TRADEMARKS LISTED ALPHABETICALLY WITH PROPRIETORS

ACRILAN ............... SOLUTIA, INC.
ACTIVENT .....................................
W.L. GORE & ASSOCIATES
ACTIVIST ................. PATAGONIA
adidas EQT TRI-QUILT.................
adidas AMERICA
AKWADYNE .............................
COMFORT TECHNOLOGIES
AKWATEK.................................
COMFORT TECHNOLOGIES
ALPHA OLEFIN...........................
AMOCO FABRICS & FIBERS
AMFIB..................... PEARL IZUMI
AQUAGUARD ............... ROTOFIL
ARCTIC FLEECE ..... MENRA MILLS
AZUREAN ................ ICON U.S.A.
BAGDAD ...........TRAVIS TEXTILES
BERBER BY GLENOIT .................
GLENOIT MILLS, INC.
BIO DRI ...................... NAUTILUS
BREATHABLES ...........................
GILDA MARX
BURLINGTON COMPOSITE
TECHNOLOGY ...........................
BURLINGTON
PERFORMANCE FABRICS
CALTECH ........ UNITIKA AMERICA
CAMBRELLE ................... FAYTEX
CANARI THERMO FLEECE...........
CANARI
CAPILENE ................ PATAGONIA
CAPROLAN ................................
ALLIED SIGNAL FIBERS
CAPTIMA....................................
ALLIED SIGNAL FIBERS
CAPTIVA ...................................
ALLIED SIGNAL FIBERS
CELANESE ACETATE ..................
CELANESE
CHINELLA ............. MENRA MILLS

CHINELLA LITE ....... MENRA MILLS
CITIFLEECE .............. DYERSBURG
CLEERSPAN ..... GLOBE MFG. CO.
CLIMA F.I.T. ........................ NIKE
CLIMAGUARD .............. ROTOFIL
CLOUD 9 FLEECE ... PEARL IZUMI
CMC ........................... INSPORT
COMFORMAX IB .......... DUPONT
COMFORMAX IB STRETCH
DUPONT
COMFORTEX ............. CHARBERT
COMFORTREL ............ WELLMAN
COMPREXX .......... DARLINGTON
COOLMAX ................... DUPONT
CORDURA PLUS ........... DUPONT
COTTONWIQUE ...COVILLE, INC.
COVILLE'S AUTHENTIC
MICROSTOP .........COVILLE, INC.
CYSTAR ........... STERLING FIBERS
DARLEXX .............. DARLINGTON
DARLEXX SUPERSKIN .................
DARLINGTON
DARLEXX THERMALASTIC ...........
DARLINGTON
DAZZLE FABRIC..........................
AMES TEXTILE CORP.
DENSIFIED BATTING ..................
BONDED FIBERS & QUILTING
DERMIZAX ....................... TORAY
DERMOFLEX ... CONSOLTEX, INC.
DESTINY ............TRAVIS TEXTILES
DIAMONDBACK ..........................
AMES TEXTILE CORP.
DORLASTAN ........... BAYER CORP.
DRALON ................ BAYER CORP.
DRI F.I.T. ............................. NIKE
DRI-LEX........................... FAYTEX
DRI-LEX AERO-SPACER ..... FAYTEX
DRI-LEX FLEECE ............. FAYTEX

143

# TRADEMARKS LISTED ALPHABETICALLY WITH PROPRIETORS

DRICLIME .................... MARMOT
DRILAYER ..... MOVING COMFORT
DRYLINE ...................... MILLIKEN
DRYLINER .................... INSPORT
DRYLOFT ..................................
      W.L. GORE & ASSOCIATES
dryskin ................... SCHOELLER
DRYSPORT ................... INSPORT
DRYWICK ......... adidas AMERICA
DURAKNIT ... YARRINGTON MILLS
DURA SPUN ........... SOLUTIA, INC.
DUREPEL ..................................
      BURLINGTON
      PERFORMANCE FABRICS
DUREPEL 1000 ........................
      BURLINGTON
      PERFORMANCE FABRICS
dynamic ................. SCHOELLER
dynatec .................. SCHOELLER
E.C.O. LITE ............. DYERSBURG
E.C.O. .................... DYERSBURG
E.C.T. ........................... LIBERTY
ECLIPSE ... ALLIED SIGNAL FIBERS
ECOPILE ...................... DRAPER
ECOPILE II ................... DRAPER
ECOTHERM ............................
      ALBANY INTERNATIONAL
ECOWOOL ............. DYERSBURG
ENTRANT GII ................... TORAY
EPICAL ......... SOMITEX PRINTERS
ESP ............................... TREVIRA
EXOSKIN ..................................
      ENTERPRISE COATINGS
EXPEL ................. GRANITEVILLE
FIELDSENSOR ................. TORAY
FILA 5 .......................... FILA USA
FILA TECH .................... FILA USA

FITNESS SLIMMERS ...................
      DANSKIN , INC.
FORTREL ................... WELLMAN
FORTREL ECOSPUN ... WELLMAN
FORTREL MICROSPUN WELLMAN
GLENAURA ................. GLENOIT
GLENPILE ................... GLENOIT
GLOSPAN ....... GLOBE MFG. CO.
GORE-TEX ...............................
      W.L. GORE & ASSOCIATES
GORE-TEX IMMERSION .............
      W.L. GORE & ASSOCIATES
GORE-TEX OCEAN TECHNOLOGY
      W.L. GORE & ASSOCIATES
GORE WINDSTOPPER ...............
      W.L. GORE & ASSOCIATES
$H_2$NO PLUS .............. PATAGONIA
$H_2$NO STORM .......... PATAGONIA
$H_2$OFF ............................ TORAY
HELLY-TECH CLASSIC .................
      HELLY-HANSEN
HELLY-TECH LIGHTNING ............
      HELLY-HANSEN
HELLY-TECH PRO .......................
      HELLY-HANSEN
HIGHLANDER ...... COVILLE, INC.
HIGHLANDER PLUS ...................
      COVILLE, INC.
HOLLOFIL .................... DUPONT
HOLLOFIL II ................. DUPONT
HYDRASUEDE ............. INSPORT
HYDRO FLAME ........................
      NATIONAL DYEWORKS
HYDRO VINYL ..........................
      NATIONAL DYEWORKS
HYDROFIL II ............................
      ALLIED SIGNAL FIBERS

HYDROFLEX .. CONSOLTEX, INC.
HYDROMOVE .............................
REEBOK INTERNATIONAL
HYDROTHANE ...........................
NATIONAL DYEWORKS
illumiNITE ...................................
REFLECTIVE TECHNOLOGIES
INNOVA ....................................
AMOCO FABRICS & FIBERS
inSIGHT ....................... INSPORT
INTERA ........................... INTERA
K-KOTE ..... KENYON INDUSTRIES
keprotec ................. SCHOELLER
keprotec with INOX . SCHOELLER
KINDERFLEECE ....... DYERSBURG
KLAY-KOTE ..................................
KENYON INDUSTRIES
LIFA ACTIVE ........ HELLY-HANSEN
LIFA ARCTIC ........ HELLY-HANSEN
LIFA ATHLETIC ..... HELLY-HANSEN
LOOPNIT ........ MONTEREY MILLS
LYCRA ........................... DUPONT
LYCRA POWER ............. DUPONT
MAX .............. CONSOLTEX, INC.
MCS............................................
BURLINGTON
PERFORMANCE FABRICS
MCT .......... MOVING COMFORT
MEMBRAIN ................. MARMOT
MICRO MESH ..............................
AMES TEXTILE CORP.
MICROSUPPLEX ........... DUPONT
MICROART ................... UNITIKA
MICROFT CONDENIER ..... TEIJIN
MICRO-LOFT ............... DUPONT
MICROMATTIQUE ........ DUPONT
MICROMATTIQUE MX ... DUPONT
MICROMATTIQUE XF .... DUPONT
MICRO-PLUSH ...........................
MONTEREY MILLS

MICROSAFE ACETATE .................
CELANESE
MICROSELECT .............. DUPONT
MICROSUPREME .......................
STERLING FIBERS
MICROTEP-25 ........... TYR SPORT
N/SL8 ............ MONTEREY MILLS
NATUREXX ........... DARLINGTON
NEOPRENE ................................
DUPONT DOW ELASTOMERS
NORDIC SPIRIT ...........................
HUNTINGDON MILLS (CAN.)
NU BLEND .... RUSSELL ATHLETIC
P.C.R. ...................... PATAGONIA
P.E.F. ...................... PATAGONIA
PERMIA ........ SOMITEX PRINTERS
PHIN-TECH ............ PEARL IZUMI
PNEUMATIC ............ PATAGONIA
POLARGUARD 3D .....................
TREVIRA
POLARGUARD HV .....................
TREVIRA
POLARTEC 100 SERIES ..............
MALDEN
POLARTEC 100 SERIES BIPOLAR
MALDEN
POLARTEC 200 SERIES ..............
MALDEN
POLARTEC 200 SERIES BIPOLAR
MALDEN
POLARTEC 300 SERIES ..............
MALDEN
POLARTEC 300 SERIES BIPOLAR
MALDEN
POLARTEC MICRO SERIES ..........
MALDEN
POLARTEC POWERSTRETCH ......
MALDEN

# TRADEMARKS LISTED ALPHABETICALLY WITH PROPRIETORS

POLARTEC THERMAL STRETCH ..
MALDEN

POLARTEC WINDBLOC ..............
MALDEN

PRIMALOFT ..............................
ALBANY INTERNATIONAL

PRO-BRITE ...............................
AMES TEXTILE CORP.

PROOF ACE ... UNITIKA AMERICA

PROPILE ............ HELLY-HANSEN

PROSPIN ...............................
NORTH POINT SPTSWR. (CONE)

QUALLOFIL ................. DUPONT

QUICK WICK ...........................
SUMMIT KNITTING MILLS

RADIATOR COLLECTION ...........
RUSSELL ATHLETIC

REACT .............. CONVERSE, INC.

REPLAY ......................... LIBERTY

REPLEX ........................... TORAY

REPLEX LIGHT ................. TORAY

RHINO CLOTH .........................
THOMASTON MILLS

SALUS ........................ FILAMENT
FIBER TECHNOLOGIES, INC

SATIN PRO MESH .....................
AMES TEXTILE CORP.

SILENZZ ................. GLEN RAVEN

skifans ..................... SCHOELLER

SKINFIT ........................ LA LAME

SNO-TEC .............. DORMA MILLS

SPANDURA ..............................
H. WARSHOW & SONS

SPANDURA FLEX-TEX ................
H. WARSHOW & SONS

SPANDURA II ............................
H. WARSHOW & SONS

SPECTRA ............. ALLIED SIGNAL

SPECTRA/SOLUTION 7 ..............
TRAVIS TEXTILES

SPORTOUCH NYLON .......... BASF

STORM F.I.T. ...................... NIKE

STORMBREAKER .. HELLY-HANSEN

STORM-TECH ...........................
BROOKWOOD COMPANIES, INC.

stretchlight .............. SCHOELLER

STUNNER ...................... TORAY

STUNNER QD ................. TORAY

SUPER MICROFT .............. TEIJIN

SUPERLOC ..............................
LIBERTY FABRICS, INC.

SUPERSKIN ..............................
DARLINGTON FABRICS CORP.

SUPPLEX ..................... DUPONT

SYMPATEX ............. AKZO NOBEL

SYMPATEX WINDLINER ..............
AKZO NOBEL

SYNCHILLA .............. PATAGONIA

SYNSATION .............. DYERSBURG

T3 ............... MOVING COMFORT

TACKLE II/GUARDIAN ................
CONSOLTEX, INC.

TACTEL ....................... DUPONT

TACTEL-AQUATOR ........ DUPONT

TEFLON ....................... DUPONT

TELAR ............... FILAMENT FIBER TECHNOLOGIES, INC
TENCEL ................ COURTAULDS
THERMA F.I.T. ..................... NIKE
THERMA FLEECE ..... PEARL IZUMI
THERMASTAT .............. DUPONT
THERMOLITE .............. DUPONT
THERMOLITE EXTREME  DUPONT
THERMOLOFT.............. DUPONT
THINSULATE ........................ 3M
THINSULATE LITE LOFT ......... 3M
THINSULATE ULTRA INSULATION 3M
TIDAL WAVE ... CONSOLTEX, INC.
TORAYDELFY 2000 .......... TORAY
TOUGHTEK ................................. HARRISON TECHNOLOGIES
TREVIRA ESP ................. TREVIRA
TREVIRA FINESSE ........... TREVIRA
TREVIRA MICRO ............. TREVIRA
TREVIRA MICRONESSE ... TREVIRA
TREVIRA MICROTHERM .. TREVIRA
TRIAD ......................................... HARRISON TECHNOLOGIES
TRIPHIBIAN ................... INSPORT
TRIPLE POINT CERAMIC ............. LOWE ALPINE
ULTRA MANIAC ............. INSPORT
ULTRA TOUCH ................... BASF
ULTRASENSOR ........ PEARL IZUMI
ULTREX ....................................... BURLINGTON PERFORMANCE FABRICS

VAPEX .... ENTERPRISE COATINGS
VERSATECH ................................. BURLINGTON PERFORMANCE FABRICS
VIPER CLOTH ........................... THOMASTON MILLS
VISA ........................... MILLIKEN
WB-formula ............. SCHOELLER
WB-formula EXTREME ............... SCHOELLER
WB-400 ................... SCHOELLER
WHIRL WIND .. CONSOLTEX, INC.
WINDBRAKE ............................. HARRISON TECHNOLOGIES
WINNING COMFORT ..... LIBERTY
WORSTERLON ............. MILLIKEN
YUKON 2000 ............................. HUNTINGDON MILLS (CAN.)
YUKON FLEECE ......................... HUNTINGDON MILLS (CAN.)
YUKON LIGHTS ......................... HUNTINGDON MILLS (CAN.)
YUKON PROTEC ......................... HUNTINGDON MILLS (CAN.)
ZEFSPORT .......................... BASF

# PROPRIETORS LISTED ALPHABETICALLY WITH TRADEMARKS

# PROPRIETORS LISTED ALPHABETICALLY WITH TRADEMARKS

# PROPRIETORS LISTED ALPHABETICALLY WITH TRADEMARKS

DANSKIN , INC. ..........................
FITNESS SLIMMERS

DARLINGTON FABRICS CORP. .....
COMPREXX
DARLEXX
DARLEXX SUPERSKIN
DARLEXX THERMALASTIC
NATUREXX

DORMA MILLS ..........................
SNO-TEC

DRAPER KNITTING CO. ..............
ECOPILE
ECOPILE II

DUPONT de NEMOURS & CO., INC.
COMFORMAX IB
COMFORMAX IB STRETCH
COOLMAX
CORDURA PLUS
HOLLOFIL
HOLLOFIL II
LYCRA
LYCRA POWER
MICRO-LOFT
MICROMATTIQUE
MICROMATTIQUE MX
MICROMATTIQUE XF
MICROSELECT
MICRO SUPPLEX
QUALLOFIL
SUPPLEX
TACTEL
TACTEL-AQUATOR
TEFLON
THERMASTAT
THERMOLITE
THERMOLITE EXTREME
THERMOLOFT

DUPONT DOW ELASTOMERS .....
NEOPRENE

DYERSBURG FABRICS, INC. .........
CITIFLEECE
E.C.O. LITE
E.C.O.
ECOWOOL
EXOSKIN
KINDERFLEECE
SYNSATION

ENTERPRISE COATINGS ..............
VAPEX

FAYTEX ......................................
CAMBRELLE
DRI-LEX
DRI-LEX
AERO-SPACER
DRI-LEX FLEECE

FILA USA, INC. ..........................
FILA 5
FILA TECH

FILAMENT FIBER
TECHNOLOGIES, INC .................
SALUS
TELAR

GILDA MARX, DIVISION,
BESTFORM INC. ........................
BREATHABLES

GLEN RAVEN ............................
SILENZZ

GLENOIT MILLS, INC. .................
BERBER BY GLENOIT
GLENAURA
GLENPILE

GLOBE MFG. CO. ......................
GLOSPAN
CLEERSPAN

GRANITEVILLE/AVONDALE
COMPANY ................................
EXPEL

H. WARSHOW & SONS ...............
SPANDURA
SPANDURA II
SPANDURA FLEX-TEX

HARRISON TECHNOLOGIES .......
TOUGHTEK
TRIAD
WINDBRAKE

HELLY-HANSEN, INC. .................
HELLY-TECH CLASSIC
HELLY-TECH PRO
HELLY-TECH LIGHTNING
LIFA ACTIVE
LIFA ARCTIC
LIFA ATHLETIC
PROPILE
STORMBREAKER

HUNTINGDON MILLS (CAN.), LTD.
NORDIC SPIRIT
YUKON 2000
YUKON FLEECE
YUKON LIGHTS
YUKON PROTEC

ICON, U.S.A. ..............................
AZUREAN

INSPORT ...................................
CMC
DRYLINER
DRYSPORT
HYDRASUEDE
inSIGHT
TRIPHIBIAN
ULTRA MANIAC

INTERA ......................................
INTERA

KENYON INDUSTRIES .................
K-KOTE
KLAY KOTE

LALAME ....................................
SKINFIT

LIBERTY FABRICS ........................
E.C.T.
REPLAY
WINNING COMFORT
SUPERLOC

LOWE ALPINE ............................
TRIPLE POINT CERAMIC

MALDEN MILLS INDUSTRIES .......
POLARTEC 100 SERIES
POLARTEC 100 SERIES BIPOLAR
POLARTEC 200 SERIES
POLARTEC 200 SERIES BIPOLAR
POLARTEC 300 SERIES
POLARTEC 300 SERIES BIPOLAR
POLARTEC MICRO SERIES
POLARTEC POWERSTRETCH
POLARTEC THERMAL STRETCH
POLARTEC WINDBLOC

MARMOT ...................................
DRICLIME
MEMBRAIN

MENRA MILLS ............................
ARCTIC FLEECE
CHINELLA
CHINELLA LITE

PROPRIETORS LISTED ALPHABETICALLY WITH TRADEMARKS

# PROPRIETORS LISTED ALPHABETICALLY WITH TRADEMARKS

MILLIKEN & COMPANY ...............
DRYLINE
VISA
WORSTERLON
MONTEREY MILLS ......................
LOOPNIT
MICROPLUSH
N/SL8
MOVING COMFORT, INC. ..........
DRILAYER
MCT
T3
NATIONAL DYEWORKS ..............
HYDRO FLAME
HYDRO VINYL
HYDROTHANE
NAUTILUS WEAR INTERNATIONAL
BIO DRI
NIKE ..........................................
CLIMA F.I.T.
DRI F.I.T.
STORM F.I.T.
THERMA F.I.T.
NORTH POINT SPTSWR. .............
PROSPIN
OUTLAST TECHNOLOGIES INC. ...
OUTLAST
PATAGONIA, INC. ......................
ACTIVIST
CAPILENE
H$_2$NO PLUS
H$_2$NO STORM
P.C.R.
P.E.F.
PNEUMATIC
SYNCHILLA

PEARL IZUMI TECHNICAL WEAR .
AMFIB
CLOUD 9 FLLECE
PHIN-TECH
THERMA FLEECE
ULTRASENSOR
REEBOK INTERNATIONAL, LTD. ..
HYDROMOVE
REFLECTIVE TECHNOLOGIES .....
illumiNITE
ROTOFIL ....................................
AQUAGUARD
CLIMAGUARD
RUSSELL ATHLETIC ....................
NU BLEND
RADIATOR COLLECTION
SCHOELLER TEXTIL U.S.A. INC. ...
SCHOELLER dryskin
SCHOELLER dynamic
SCHOELLER dynatec
SCHOELLER keprotec
SCHOELLER keprotec with Inox
SCHOELLER stretchlight
SCHOELLER WB formula
WB formula Extreme
SCHOELLER WB400
SOLUTIA, INC. ...........................
ACRILAN
DURA SPUN

PROPRIETORS LISTED ALPHABETICALLY WITH TRADEMARKS

# TRADEMARKS GROUPED ACCORDING TO PRIMARY AND SECONDARY USE CATEGORIES

This section lists all trademarked products grouped according to their use and position in the Dictionary. They are grouped both as to **where you can find their full primary description**, as well as listing products with **secondary** properties of the same type found elsewhere in the Dictionary.

157

# TRADEMARKS GROUPED ACCORDING TO PRIMARY AND SECONDARY USE CATEGORIES

## FIBERS

ACRILAN .............. SOLUTIA, INC.
ALPHA OLEFIN ...........................
         AMOCO FABRICS & FIBERS
CAPROLAN ...............................
         ALLIED SIGNAL FIBERS
CAPTIMA.................................
         ALLIED SIGNAL FIBERS
CAPTIVA ..................................
         ALLIED SIGNAL FIBERS
CELANESE ACETATE ...................
         CELANESE ACETATE
COMFORTREL ............ WELLMAN
COOLMAX .................. DU PONT
CORDURA PLUS .......... DU PONT
CYSTAR AF ....... STERLING FIBERS
DORLASTAN ........... BAYER CORP.
DRALON ................. BAYER CORP.
DURASPUN ........... SOLUTIA, INC.
ECLIPSE ... ALLIED SIGNAL FIBERS
FORTREL.................... WELLMAN
FORTREL ECOSPUN ... WELLMAN
FORTREL MICROSPUN  WELLMAN
GLOSPAN ....... GLOBE MFG, CO.
HYDROFIL ...............................
         ALLIED SIGNAL FIBERS
HYDROFIL II .............................
         ALLIED SIGNAL FIBERS
INNOVA ...................................
         AMOCO FABRICS & FIBERS
LYCRA ....................... DU PONT
MICROMATTIQUE ....... DU PONT
MICROMATTIQUE MX .. DU PONT
MICROMATTIQUE XF ... DU PONT
MICROSAFE ACETATE ................
         CELANESE ACETATE
MICROSELECT ............ DU PONT
MICROSUPPLEX .......... DU PONT
MICROSUPREME .......................
         STERLING FIBERS

P.C.R. ...................... PATAGONIA
PROSPIN .......................... CONE
SALUS ......................................
    FILAMENT FIBER TECHNOLOGIES
SPORTOUCH NYLON .......... BASF
SUPPLEX .................... DU PONT
TACTEL ..................... DU PONT
TELAR ......................................
    FILAMENT FIBER TECHNOLOGIES
TENCEL ............... COURTAULDS
THERMASTAT ............. DU PONT
TREVIRA ........................ TREVIRA
TREVIRA ESP ................. TREVIRA
TREVIRA FINESSE ........... TREVIRA
TREVIRA MICRO ............ TREVIRA
TREVIRA MICRONESSE ... TREVIRA
TREVIRA MICROTHERM .. TREVIRA
ULTRA TOUCH ................... BASF
ZEFSPORT ......................... BASF

## INSULATION

ACTIVIST ................. PATAGONIA
adidas EQT TRI-QUILT ....... adidas
ARCTIC FLEECE ..... MENRA MILLS
BERBER BY GLENOIT ................
             GLENOIT MILLS
CHINELLA ............. MENRA MILLS
CHINELLA LITE ...... MENRA MILLS
CITIFLEECE ............................
         DYERSBURG FABRICS
CLOUD 9 FLEECE ... PEARL IZUMI
DENSIFIED BATTING ..................
    BONDED FIBERS & QUILTING
E.C.O. ....... DYERSBURG FABRICS
E.C.O. LITE .............. DYERSBURG
ECOPILE ........ DRAPER KNITTING
ECOPILE II ..... DRAPER KNITTING
ECOTHERM ..............................
         ALBANY INTERNATIONAL
E.C.O. WOOL ...........................
            DYERSBURG

# TRADEMARKS GROUPED ACCORDING TO PRIMARY AND SECONDARY USE CATEGORIES

GLENAURA ......... GLENOIT MILLS
GLENPILE .................... GLENOIT
HIGHLANDER ....... COVILLE, INC.
HIGHLANDER PLUS ...................
COVILLE INC.
HOLLOFIL ................... DU PONT
HOLLOFIL II ............... DU PONT
KINDERFLEECE ..........................
DYERSBURG FABRICS
LIFA ARCTIC ........ HELLY-HANSEN
MICROART .................... UNITIKA
MICRO-LOFT ............... DU PONT
MICROPLUSH .. MONTEREY MILLS
N/SL8 ............. MONTEREY MILLS
NEOPRENE ................................
DU PONT DOW ELASTOMERS
NORDIC SPIRIT ..........................
HUNTINGDON MILLS (CAN)
OUTLAST ....................................
OUTLAST TECHNOLOGIES
POLARGUARD 3D .......... TREVIRA
POLARGUARD HV .......... TREVIRA
POLARTEC .......... MALDEN MILLS
POLARTEC 100 SERIES ...............
MALDEN MILLS
POLARTEC 200 SERIES ...............
MALDEN MILLS
POLARTEC 200 BI-POLAR ...........
MALDEN MILLS
POLARTEC 300 SERIES ...............
MALDEN MILLS
POLARTEC 300 BI-POLAR ...........
MALDEN MILLS
POLARTEC MICRO SERIES ...........
MALDEN MILLS
POLARTEC POWERSTRETCH .......
MALDEN MILLS
POLARTEC THERMAL SERIES .......
MALDEN MILLS
PRIMALOFT ...............................
ALBANY INTERNATIONAL

PROPILE .............. HELLY-HANSEN
QUALLOFIL ................. DU PONT
REPELEX ......................... TORAY
REPLEX LITE ................... TORAY
SNO-TEC ...... DORMA MILLS, INC.
THERMA F.I.T. ............. NIKE, INC.
THERMA FLEECE ..... PEARL IZUMI
THERMOLITE ............. DU PONT
THERMOLITE EXTREME ..............
DU PONT
THERMOLOFT ............. DU PONT
THINSULATE ......................... 3M
THINSULATE LITE LOFT ......... 3M
THINSULATE ULTRA INSULATION
3M
WORSTERLON ... MILLIKEN & CO.
YUKON 2000 .............................
HUNTINGDON MILLS (CAN)
YUKON FLEECE ........................
HUNTINGDON MILLS (CAN)
YUKON PROTEC .......................
HUNTINGDON MILLS (CAN)

## Products listed here have INSULATION as a secondary property.

ALPHA OLEFIN ...............AMOCO
CANARI THERMO FLEECE ..........
CANARI CYCLE WEAR
COMFORTEX ............. CHARBERT
HYDROMOVE ...........................
REEBOK INTERNATIONAL
INNOVA ........................AMOCO
LIFA ATHLETIC ..... HELLY-HANSEN
DRICLIME .................... MARMOT
MCT ........... MOVING COMFORT.
PHIN-TECH ............. PEARL IZUMI
POLARGUARD ................TREVIRA
POLARTEC 100 BI-POLAR ...........
MALDEN MILLS
SCHOELLER skifans .. SCHOELLER

# TRADEMARKS GROUPED ACCORDING TO PRIMARY AND SECONDARY USE CATEGORIES

SCHOELLER stretchlite .............. SCHOELLER

SCHOELLER WB 400 ................. SCHOELLER

SPANDURA® FLEX-TEX ............... H. WARSHOW& SONS

SYMPATEX ................................ AKZO NOBEL-SYMPATEX

TELAR ...................................... FILAMENT FIBER TECHNOLOGIES

TREVIRA MICROTHERM ............. TREVIRA

YUKON LIGHTS ......................... HUNTINGDON MILLS (CAN)

## MOISTURE MANAGEMENT

AKWADYNE .............................. COMFORT TECHNOLOGIES

AKWATEK .................................. COMFORT TECHNOLOGIES

BAGDAD ...........TRAVIS TEXTILES

BIO DRI ............ NAUTILUS WEAR

BREATHABLES ......... GILDA MARX

CAMBRELLE .................... FAYTEX

CAPILENE ................ PATAGONIA

CMC .......................... INSPORT

COMFORTEX ............. CHARBERT

COTTONWIQUE ...COVILLE, INC.

DRI-CLIME ................... MARMOT

DRILAYER .....MOVING COMFORT

DRI F.I.T. ..................... NIKE, INC.

DRI-LEX.......................... FAYTEX

DRI-LEX AERO-SPACER ..... FAYTEX

DRI-LEX FLEECE ............. FAYTEX

DRYLINE ........... MILLIKEN & CO.

DRYLINER .................... INSPORT

DRYSPORT .................... INSPORT

DRYWICK ........................ adidas

FIELDSENSOR ................. TORAY

HYDRASUEDE .............. INSPORT

HYDROMOVE .............. REEBOK

INTERA ......................... INTERA

LIFA ACTIVE ........ HELLY-HANSEN

LIFA ATHLETIC ..... HELLY-HANSEN

LOOPKNIT ...... MONTEREY MILLS

MAX .............. CONSOLTEX, INC.

MCS ..................... BURLINGTON PERFORMANCE FABRICS

NATUREXX ................................. DARLINGTON FABRICS

PHIN-TECH ............ PEARL IZUMI

POLARTEC 100 BI-POLAR ........... MALDEN

QUIKWICK ..... SUMMIT KTG. MILLS

RADIATOR ..... RUSSELL ATHLETIC

SCHOELLER dryskin . SCHOELLER

SCHOELLER dynamic ................. SCHOELLER

SYNCHILLA ............. PATAGONIA

T3 ...............MOVING COMFORT

TACTEL AQUATOR....... DU PONT

ULTRASENSOR ........ PEARL IZUMI

WINNING COMFORT ................. LIBERTY FABRICS

YUKON LIGHTS ... HUNTINGDON

### Products listed here have MOISTURE MANAGEMENT as a secondary property

ACRILAN ..............SOLUTIA, INC.

ALPHA OLEFIN..............AMOCO

AMFIB.................... PEARL IZUMI

CANARI THERMO FLEECE CANARI

COMFORTREL........... WELLMAN

COOLMAX ................. DU PONT

COVILLE'S MICROSTOP ............. COVILLE, INC.

# TRADEMARKS GROUPED ACCORDING TO PRIMARY AND SECONDARY USE CATEGORIES

CHINELLA ............. MENRA MILLS
CHINELLA LITE ...... MENRA MILLS
DRALON ........................... BAYER
DURASPUN ........... SOLUTIA, INC.
ECOWOOL .................................
               DYERSBURG FABRICS
E.C.T. ................ LIBERTY FABRICS
FITNESS SLIMMERS ....... DANSKIN
GLENAURA ......... GLENOIT MILLS
GLENPILE ........... GLENOIT MILLS
GORE-TEX OCEAN TECHNOLOGY
                         W.L. GORE
$H_2NO$ STORM .......... PATAGONIA
HELLY-TECH CLASSIC ..................
                      HELLY-HANSEN
HELLY-TECH LIGHTNING ............
                      HELLY-HANSEN
HELLY-TECH PRO .......................
                      HELLY-HANSEN
HYDROFIL .......... ALLIED SIGNAL
INNOVA ........................ AMOCO
KINDERFLEECE .........................
               DYERSBURG FABRICS
LIFA ARCTIC ........ HELLY-HANSEN
MICROPLUSH .. MONTEREY MILLS
MICROSELECT ............. DU PONT
MICROSUPREME ........................
                     STERLING FIBERS
N/SL8 ............. MONTEREY MILLS
NORDIC SPIRIT ..........................
           HUNTINGDON MILLS (CAN)
P.E.F. ........................ PATAGONIA
POLARTEC 100 SERIES ...............
                      MALDEN MILLS
POLARTEC 300 BI-POLAR ...........
                      MALDEN MILLS
POLARTEC MICRO SERIES ...........
                      MALDEN MILLS
POLARTEC POWERSTRETCH .......
                      MALDEN MILLS

POLARTEC WINDBLOC ...............
                      MALDEN MILLS
PROPILE ............. HELLY-HANSEN
PROSPIN ..................................
      NORTH POINT SPTSWR (CONE)
SCHOELLER dynatec & dynatec
EXTREME ...................................
                        SCHOELLER
SCHOELLER skifans .. SCHOELLER
SCHOELLER stretchlight ............
                        SCHOELLER
SCHOELLER WB 400 .................
                        SCHOELLER
SCHOELLER WB formula ............
                        SCHOELLER
SCHOELLER WB formula EXTREME
                        SCHOELLER
SPANDURA FLEX-TEX .................
              H. WARSHOW & SONS
THERMA FLEECE ..... PEARL IZUMI
THERMASTAT ............. DU PONT
TRIPHIBIAN ................... INSPORT
ULTRA MANIAC ............. INSPORT
VISA .................. MILLIKEN & CO.
WINDBRAKE .............................
         HARRISON TECHNOLOGIES
WORSTERLON ... MILLIKEN & CO.
YUKON 2000 ............................
          HUNTINGDON MILLS (CAN)
YUKON FLEECE .......................
          HUNTINGDON MILLS (CAN)

## WATERPROOF, WINDPROOF, BUT BREATHABLE

ACTIVENT ................. W.L. GORE
AMFIB .................... PEARL IZUMI
AQUAGUARD .............. ROTOFIL
BURLINGTON COMPOSITE
TECHNOLOGY .........................
     BURLINGTON PERFORMANCE FABRICS

# TRADEMARKS GROUPED ACCORDING TO PRIMARY AND SECONDARY USE CATEGORIES

CALTECH ........ UNITIKA AMERICA
CANARI THERMO FLEECE...........
PATAGONIA
CLIMA F.I.T. ............... NIKE, INC.
CLIMAGUARD ............... ROTOFIL
COMFORTMAX IB ....... DU PONT
COMFORTMAX IB STRETCH ........
DU PONT
DARLEXX . DARLINGTON FABRICS
DERMIZAX ...................... TORAY
DERMOFLEX ... CONSOLTEX, INC.
DESTINY ............TRAVIS TEXTILES
DRYLOFT .................. W.L. GORE
DUREPEL ........................
BURLINGTON PERFORMANCE
DUREPEL 1000 ........................
BURLINGTON PERFORMANCE
ENTRANT GII .................... TORAY
EPICAL .........................SOMITEX
EXOSKIN...................................
ENTERPRISE COATINGS
FILA TECH .................... FILA USA
GORE-TEX .................. W.L. GORE
GORE-TEX IMMERSION ..............
W.L. GORE
GORE-TEX OCEAN
TECHNOLOGY ...........................
W.L. GORE
GORE WINDSTOPPER ................
W.L. GORE
H₂NO PLUS .............. PATAGONIA
H₂NO STORM ............................
PATAGONIA
H₂OFF ........................... TORAY
HELLY-TECH CLASSIC ..................
HELLY-HANSEN
HELLY-TECH LIGHTNING ............
HELLY-HANSEN
HELLY-TECH PRO .......................
HELLY-HANSEN

HYDROFLEX ... CONSOLTEX, INC.
HYDROTHANE ...........................
NATIONAL DYEWORKS
HYDRO VINYL ...........................
NATIONAL DYEWORKS
K-KOTE ...... KENYON INDUSTRIES
KLAY-KOTE ...............................
KENYON INDUSTRIES
MEMBRAIN .................. MARMOT
MICROFT CONDENIER ...... TEIJIN
P.E.F. ........................ PATAGONIA
PERMIA ........................SOMITEX
PNEUMATIC ............ PATAGONIA
POLARTEC WINDBLOC...............
MALDEN MILLS
PROOF ACE .... UNITIKA AMERICA
SCHOELLER skifans .. SCHOELLER
SCHOELLER stretchlite................
SCHOELLER
SCHOELLER WB 400 ..................
SCHOELLER
SCHOELLER WB formula ............
SCHOELLER
SCHOELLER WB formula EXTREME
SCHOELLER
SKIN FIT ......................... LALAME
STORM F.I.T. ............... NIKE, INC.
STORM-TECH ....... BROOKWOOD
STORMBREAKER .. HELLY-HANSEN
SUPER MICROFT .............. TEIJIN
SYMPATEX..................................
AKZO NOBEL SYMPATEX
SYMPATEX WINDLINER...............
AKZO NOBEL SYMPATEX
TORAYDELFY 2000 .......... TORAY
TRIAD .........................................
HARRISON TECHNOLOGIES
TRIPHIBIAN ................... INSPORT
TRIPLE POINT CERAMIC ..............
LOWE ALPINE

# TRADEMARKS GROUPED ACCORDING TO PRIMARY AND SECONDARY USE CATEGORIES

ULTRA MANIAC ............. INSPORT
ULTREX ........................................
      BURLINGTON PERFORMANCE
      FABRICS
VAPEX .... ENTERPRISE COATINGS
VERSATECH ...............................
      BURLINGTON PERFORMANCE
      FABRICS
WHIRL WIND .. CONSOLTEX, INC.
WINDBRAKE ..............................
      HARRISON TECHNOLOGIES

## Products listed here have WATERPROOF/ WINDPROOF/ BREATHABLE as a secondary property

ARTIC FLEECE ....... MENRA MILLS
DARLEXX THERMALATIC .............
      DARLINGTON FABRICS
E.C.O. ....... DYERSBURG FABRICS
E.C.O. LITE ...............................
      DYERSBURG FABRICS
ECOPILE ........ DRAPER KNITTING
ECOTHERM ...............................
      ALBANY INTERNATIONAL
GLENAURA ......... GLENOIT MILLS
GLEN PILE .......... GLENOIT MILLS
MICROART ...... UNITIKA AMERICA
MICROTEP-25 ........... TYR SPORT
NORDIC SPIRIT .........................
      HUNTINGDON MILLS (CAN)
POLARTEC 300 SERIES ...............
      MALDEN MILLS
POLARTEC MICRO SERIES
      MALDEN MILLS
POLARTEC THERMAL STRETCH ...
      MALDEN MILLS
PRIMALOFT ...............................
      ALBANY INTERNATIONAL

SATIN PRO MESH .. AMES TEXTILE
SILENZZ ................. GLEN RAVEN
SPANDURA ...............................
      H. WARSHOW & SONS
SPANDURA II..............................
      H. WARSHOW & SONS
TIDAL WAVE ... CONSOLTEX, INC.
YUKON 2000 ...........................
      HUNTINGDON MILLS (CAN)

## STRETCH

COMPREXX ...............................
      DARLINGTON FABRICS
DARLEXX SUPERSKIN
      ................
      DARLINGTON FABRICS
DARLEXX THERMALASTIC ...........
      DARLINGTON FABRICS
E.C.T. ................ LIBERTY FABRICS
ESP ................................ TREVIRA
FITNESS SLIMMERS ....... DANSKIN
MCT ............ MOVING COMFORT
NEOPRENE ...............................
      DUPONT DOW ELASTOMERS
POLARTEC POWER STRETCH ......
      MALDEN MILLS
REPLAY ............. LIBERTY FABRICS
SPANDURA ...............................
      H. WARSHOW & SONS
SPANDURA FLEX-TEX .................
      H. WARSHOW & SONS
SPANDURA II..............................
      H. WARSHOW & SONS
SUPERLOC ........ LIBERTY FABRICS
SYNSATION ...............................
      DYERSBURG FABRICS

## Products listed here have STRETCH as a secondary property

amFIB .................... PEARL IZUMI

CANARI THERMO FLEECE........... CANARI

CLOUD 9 FLEECE ... PEARL IZUMI

DARLEXX . DARLINGTON FABRICS

DERMIZAX ...................... TORAY

DRILAYER .....MOVING COMFORT

EXOSKIN.................................. ENTERPRISE COATINGS

LIFA ACTIVE ................. MARMOT

MARMOT DRICLIME ..... MARMOT

MARMOT MEMBRAIN ... MARMOT

MICROTEP-25 ............ TYR SPORT

NATUREXX............................... DARLINGTON FABRICS

PNEUMATIC ............. PATAGONIA

POLARTEC THERMAL STRETCH ... MALDEN MILLS

SCHOELLER dryskin . SCHOELLER

SCHOELLER dynamic & dynamic EXTREME .................................... SCHOELLER

SCHOELLER skifans .. SCHOELLER

SCHOELLER stretchlite................ SCHOELLER

SCHOELLER WB 400 .................. SCHOELLER

SCHOELLER WB formula & EXTREME .................................... SCHOELLER

SKIN FIT ......................... LALAME

T3 ...............MOVING COMFORT

THERMA FLEECE ..... PEARL IZUMI

TRIPHIBIAN ................... INSPORT

ULTRASENSOR ........ PEARL IZUMI

VAPEX .... ENTERPRISE COATINGS

WINNING COMFORT ................. LIBERTY FABRICS

YUKON PROTEC ........................ HUNTINGDON MILLS (CAN)

## SPECIAL PRODUCTS
### Abrasion Resistance

DURAKNIT ................................. YARRINGTON MILLS, CORP.

RHINO CLOTH .......................... THOMASTON MILLS

SCHOELLER - dynatec ................ SCHOELLER

SCHOELLER - keprotec ............... SCHOELLER

SCHOELLER - keprotec with INOX SCHOELLER

SPECTRA/SOLUTION 7 ............... TRAVIS TEXTILES

TACKLE II/ GUARDIAN ................ CONSOLTEX, INC.

TIDAL WAVE ... CONSOLTEX, INC.

TOUGHTEK ................................ HARRISON TECHNOLOGIES

### Anti-Microbial

COVILLE'S AM MICROSTOP ........ COVILLE, INC.

### Compression

LYCRA POWER ........... DU PONT

### Cushioning

REACT ...................... CONVERSE

### Fashion

STUNNER ....................... TORAY

STUNNER QD ................. TORAY

FILA 5 ........................... FILA USA

### Flame Retardance

HYDRO FLAME ......................... NATIONAL DYEWORKS

### Insect Repellency

EXPEL ....................................... GRANITEVILLE FABRIC, Division of AVONDALE MILLS

165

# TRADEMARKS GROUPED ACCORDING TO PRIMARY AND SECONARY USE CATEGORIES

## Silence
SILENZZ ....... GLEN RAVEN MILLS

## Snake-Proof
VIPER CLOTH ............................
THOMASTON MILLS

## Soil & Stain Release
TEFLON ..................... DU PONT
VISA ................. MILLIKEN & CO.

## Speed
MICROTEP - 25 .......... TYR SPORT

## Team Sport
DAZZLE FABRIC .........................
AMES TEXTILES/GAME TIME
DIAMONDBACK .........................
AMES TEXTILES/GAME TIME
MICRO MESH ............................
AMES TEXTILES/GAME TIME
NU BLEND ..... RUSSELL ATHLETIC
PRO-BRITE ...............................
AMES TEXTILES/GAME TIME
SATIN PRO MESH ......................
AMES TEXTILES/GAME TIME

## Reflectance
illumiNITE ................................
reflective technologies, inc.
inSIGHT ........................ INSPORT

## Ultra Violet Light Protection
AZUREAN ................. ICON U.S.A.

## Products listed here have THE FOLLOWING SPECIAL PROPERTIES as a secondary feature

## Abrasion Resistance
BAGDAD .......... TRAVIS TEXTILES
BURLINGTON COMPOSITE

TECHNOLOGY ...........................
BURLINGTON PERFORMANCE
CALTECH ........ UNITIKA AMERICA
CAMBRELLE .................... FAYTEX
DARLEXX THERMALASTIC ...........
DARLINGTON FABRICS
DAZZLE .............. AMES TEXTILES
DRYSPORT .................... INSPORT
DURAKNIT ... YARRINGTON MILLS
EXOSKIN . ENTERPRISE COATINGS
H$_2$NO STORM .......... PATAGONIA
HYDROTHANE .........................
NATIONAL DYEWORKS
HYDRO VINYL ...........................
NATIONAL DYEWORKS
KLAY KOTE ...............................
KENYON INDUSTRIES
PNEUMATIC ............. PATAGONIA
POLARTEC 200 BI-POLAR ...........
MALDEN MILLS
POLARTEC POWERSTRETCH .......
MALDEN MILLS
PRO BRITE ...............................
AMES TEXTILES/GAME TIME
PROOF ACE .... UNITIKA AMERICA
REPLAY ............. CONVERSE, INC.
SATIN PRO MESH ......................
AMES TEXTILES
SCHOELLER dynamic ................
SCHOELLER
SCHOELLER dynamic EXTREME ..
SCHOELLER
SCHOELLER WB formula ...........
SCHOELLER
SNO-TEC ............... DORMA MILLS
SPANDURA ..............................
H. WARSHOW & SONS
SPANDURA II ...........................
H. WARSHOW & SONS

SPANDURA FLEX-TEX ................. H. WARSHOW & SONS

ULTRA MANIAC ............ INSPORT

WORSTERLON ... MILLIKEN & CO.

(Note: Nearly all synthetic fibers are abrasion resistant to a degree. Excepted are micro fibers, spandex, acetate and rayon)

## Anti-Microbial

BIO DRY ........... NAUTILUS WEAR

BREATHABLES ......... GILDA MARX

CALTECH ........ UNITIKA AMERICA

COVILLE'S AUTHENTIC MICROSTOP ............................... COVILLE, INC.

CYSTAR AF ....... STERLING FIBERS

DRI LEX .......................... FAYTEX

DRI LEX AERO-SPACER ..... FAYTEX

DRI LEX FLEECE .............. FAYTEX

DRILAYER ..... MOVING COMFORT

INNOVA ........................ AMOCO

INTERA .......................... INTERA

MICROSAFE . CELANESE ACETATE

NATUREXX ................................ DARLINGTON FABRICS

POLARTEC 100 SERIES ............... MALDEN MILLS

POLARTEC 100 BI-POLAR ........... MALDEN MILLS

POLARTEC 300 SERIES .............. MALDEN MILLS

POLARTEC 300 BI-POLAR ........... MALDEN MILLS

POLARTEC THERMAL STRETCH ... MALDEN MILLS

SALUS ........................................ FILAMENT FIBER TECHNOLOGIES

T3 .............. MOVING COMFORT

TELAR ...................................... FILAMENT FIBER TECHNOLOGIES

TRIPHIBIAN ................... INSPORT

## Flame Resistance

ECOWOOL ................................ DYERSBURG FABRICS

KINDERFLEECE ......................... DYERSBURG FABRICS

SNO-TEC .............. DORMA MILLS

## Reflectance

ULTRA MANIAC ............ INSPORT

## Silence

DESTINY ........... TRAVIS TEXTILES

TORAYDELFY 2000 .......... TORAY

## Soil & Stain Release

CITIFLEECE .................................. DYERSBURG FABRICS

DUREPEL ...................................... BURLINGTON PERFORMANCE FABRICS

INTERA .......................... INTERA

KINDERFLEECE .......................... DYERSBURG FABRICS

QUICKWICK ............................... SUMMIT KNITTING MILLS

SCHOELLER skifans ................... SCHOELLER

## Speed

DARLEXX . DARLINGTON FABRICS

SKINFIT ........................ LA LAME

SUPERSKIN ............................... DARLINGTON FABRICS

## UV Degradation Protection

EXOSKIN ..................................... ENTERPRISE COATINGS

ECLIPSE .............. ALLIED SIGNAL

# LIST OF TRADEMARK PROPRIETORS

## (ADDRESS, PHONE & FAX NUMBERS)

# LIST OF TRADEMARK PROPRIETERS

## (ADDRESS, PHONE & FAX NUMBERS)

**3M Personal Safety Products**
Building 225-4N-14
St. Paul, MN 55144
(612) 733-9781
Fax: (612) 737-5679

**adidas® America**
9605 SW Nimbus
Beaverton, OR 97008
(503) 736-5866
Fax: (503) 797-4935

**Akzo Nobel-Sympatex**
1 Merrill Industrial Drive, Suite 201
Hampton, NH 03842
(603) 929-3901
Fax: (603) 929-3905

**Albany International Corp.**
PO Box 1907
Albany, NY 12201
(518) 445-2200
Fax: (518) 445-2265

**Allied Signal, Inc.**
1411 Broadway, 39th Floor
New York, NY 10018
(212) 391-5000
Fax: (212) 391-5165

**Ames Textile Corporation**
710 Chelmsford Street
Lowell, MA 01851
(508) 454-9146
Fax: (508) 454-9148

**Amoco Fabrics & Fibers Co.**
PO Box 66
Greenville, SC 29602
(864) 627-3334
Fax: (864) 675-9873

**BASF Corporation**
1675 Broadway
New York, NY 10019
(212) 408-9700
Fax: (212) 408-9740

**Bayer Corporation**
PO Box 118088
Charleston, SC 29423-8088
(803) 820-6000
Fax: (803) 820-6592

**Bonded Fibers & Quilting**
1720 Fuller Road
West DesMoines, IO 50265
(515) 223-5668
Fax: (515) 223-2276

**Brookwood Companies, Inc.**
232 Madison Avenue
New York, NY 10016
(212) 551-0100
Fax: (212) 686-5626

**Burlington Performance Fabrics**
1345 Avenue of the Americas
New York, NY 10105
(212) 621-3570
Fax: (212) 621-1038

**Canari Cycle Wear**
10025 Huennekens Street
San Diego, CA 92121
(619) 455-8245
Fax: (619) 455-8292

**Charbert Division of NFA Corp.**
48-226 Bi-State Plaza
Old Tappan, NJ 07675
(201) 722-9749
Fax: (201) 722-1398

**Comfort Technologies, Inc.**
P.O. Box 931
Gastonia, NC 28053-0931
(704) 864-5728
Fax: (704) 853-3850

**Concept III Textile Sales, Inc.**
125 Half Mile Road
Red Bank, NJ 07701
(732) 530-1976
Fax: (732) 530-4969

**Cone Mills Corporation**
310 North Elm Street
Greensboro, NC 27410
(910) 379-6220
Fax: (910) 379-6240

**Consoltex Group, Inc.**
8555 TransCanada Highway
St Laurent, Que. H4S 1Z6,
Canada
(514) 333-8800
Fax: (514) 335-7018

# LIST OF TRADEMARK PROPRIETERS

## (ADDRESS, PHONE & FAX NUMBERS)

**Converse, Inc.**
1 Fordham Road
North Reading, MA 01864
(508) 664-1100
Fax: (508) 664-7259

**Courtaulds North America Inc.**
111 West 40th Street 34th Floor
New York, NY 10018
(212) 944-7400
Fax: (212) 944-7406

**Coville, Inc.**
8065-0 North Point Blvd.
Winston-Salem, NC 27106
(910) 759-0115
Fax: (910) 759-2229

**Danskin, Inc.**
111 West 40th Street
New York, NY 10018
(212) 764-4630
Fax: (212) 768-1638

**Darlington Fabrics Corp.**
1359 Broadway, Suite 1404
New York, NY 10018
(212) 279-7733
Fax: (212) 564-5325

**Dorma Mills**
184-10 Jamaica Avenue
Hollis, NY 11423
(212) 254-7150
Fax: (718) 264-7300

**Draper Knitting Company, Inc.**
28 Draper Lane
Canton, MA 02021
(781) 828-0029
Fax: (781) 828-3034

**DuPont De Nemours & Co., Inc.**
Barley Mill Plaza, PO Box 80025
Wilmington, DE 19880-0025
(800) 441-7515
Fax: (302) 992-4552

**DuPont Dow Elastomers L.L.C.**
4330 Allen Road
Stow, OH 44224-1094
(800) 853-5515 Ext 3
Fax: (302) 892-7390

**Dyersburg Fabrics, Inc.**
1315 East Phillip Street
Dyersburg, TN 38024
(901) 285-2323
Fax: (901) 286-3474

**Enterprise Coatings Limited**
22 Steel Street
North Smithfield, RI 02876
(401) 766-1500
Fax: (401) 767-3347

**Faytex**
185 Libby Parkway
Waymouth, MA 02189
(617) 331-9004
Fax: (617) 331-9317

**Fila, USA, Inc.**
PO Box 3000
Sparks, MD 21152-3000
(410) 773-3000
Fax: (410) 773-4973

**Filament Fiber Technology, Inc.**
571 West Lake Avenue
Bay Head, NJ 08742
(732) 295-5900
Fax: (732) 295-5910

**Gehring Textiles, Inc.**
1 West 34th Street, #1001
New York, NY 10001
(212) 279-9700
Fax: (212) 279-8381

**Gilda Marx, Division Bestform, Inc.**
1430 Broadway, Suite 1100
New York, NY 10018
(212) 921-0040
Fax: (212) 302-0359

**Glen Raven Mills, Inc.**
1831 North Park Avenue
Glen Raven, NC 27217
(910) 227-6211
Fax: (910) 226-1446

**Glenoit Corporation**
111 West 40th Street
23rd Floor
New York, NY 10018
(212) 391-3915
Fax: (212) 869-5898

**Globe Manufacturing Company**
456 Bedford Street
Fall River, MA 02720
(508) 674-3585
Fax: (508) 674-3580

**Graniteville/ Avondale Company**
PO Box 128
Graniteville, SC 29829
(803) 663-7231
Fax: (803) 663-5809

**H. Warshow & Sons, Inc.**
1375 Broadway
New York, NY 10018
(212) 921-9200
Fax: (212) 944-5704

**Harrison Technologies**
PO Box 272
Gloversville, NY 12078
(518) 725-9434
Fax: (518) 725-9634

**Helly Hansen, (US), Inc.**
17275 N.E. 67th Ct.
Redmond, WA 98052
(425) 883-8823
Fax: (425) 882-4932

**Hobbs Bonded Fibers**
200 South Commerce St.
Waco, TX 76710
(254) 741-0040
Fax: (254) 772-7238

**Huntingdon Mills Canada, Ltd.**
72 Dalhousie Street
Huntingdon, Que. J0S 1H0, Can.
(514) 264-8000
Fax: (514) 264-6921

**Icon, U.S.A.**
880 Apollo Street, Suite 235
El Segundo, CA 90245
(310) 615-0416
Fax: (310) 615-0376

**Insport International, Inc.**
1870 N. W. 173 Road
Beaverton, OR 97006-4850
(503) 645-3552
Fax: (503) 629-9455

**Intera Corporation**
PO Box 25376
Chattanooga, TN 37422-5376
(423) 892-9911
Fax: (423) 842-3037

**Kenyon Industries, Inc.**
36 Sherman Ave.
Kenyon, RI 02836
(401) 364-3400
Fax: (401) 364-6130

**Kornfli Spindale Knitting Mill, Inc.**
4000 Medford Street
Los Angeles, CA 90063
(213) 780-7700
Fax: (213) 266-1818

**LaLame, Inc.**
250 West 39th Street 4th Floor
New York, NY 10018
(212) 921-9770
Fax: (212) 302-4359

**Liberty Fabrics, Inc.**
295 Fifth Avenue
New York, NY 10016
(212) 684-3100
Fax: (212) 683-8093

**Lowe Alpine Systems, Inc.**
PO Box 1449
Broomfield, CO 80038
(303) 465-3706
Fax: (303) 465-3301

**Malden Mills Industries, Inc.**
46 Stafford Street
Lawrence, MA 01841
(978) 685-6341
Fax: (978) 659-5709

LIST OF TRADEMARK PROPRIETORS (ADDRESS, PHONE & FAX NUMBERS)

# LIST OF TRADEMARK PROPRIETERS

## (ADDRESS, PHONE & FAX NUMBERS)

**Marmot Mountain, Ltd.**
2321 Circadian Way
Santa Rosa, CA 95407
(707) 544-4590
Fax: (707) 544-1344

**Menra Mills Corporation**
201 Route 17 N
Rutherford, NJ 07070
(201) 933-6655
Fax: (201) 933-8487

**Milliken & Company**
PO Box 1926 M-132
Spartanburg, SC 29304-1926
(864) 503-2654
(864) 503-2984

**Monterey, Inc.**
PO Box 271
Janesville, WI 53547
(800) 255-9665
Fax: (608) 754-3750

**Moving Comfort, Inc.**
4500 Southgate Place
Suite 800
Chantilly, VA 20151
(703) 631-1000
Fax: (703) 631-1001

**National Dyeworks**
Route 1, Box 3, Highway 76E
Lynchburg, SC 29080
(800) 321-3931
Fax: (803) 437-2704

**Nautilus Wear International**
80 West 40th Street
Suite 42
New York, NY 10018
(212) 997-2000
Fax: (212) 997-1955

**Nike, Inc.**
1 Bowerman Drive
Beaverton, OR 97005
(503) 671-6453
Fax: (503) 671-6300

**Outlast Technologies, Inc.**
6235 Lookout Road
Boulder, CO 80301
(303) 581-0801
Fax: (303) 581-9029

**Patagonia, Inc.**
259 West Santa Clara Street
Ventura, CA 93001
(805) 643-8616
Fax: (805) 653-6355

**Pearl Izumi Technical Wear**
620 Compton Street
Broomfield, CO 80020
(303) 460-8888
Fax: (303) 466-4237

**Reebok International, Ltd.**
100 Technology Center Drive
Stoughton, MA 02072-4705
(617) 341-5000
Fax: (617) 297-4800

**Reflective Technologies, Inc.**
15 Tudor Street
Cambridge, MA 02139
(617) 497-6171
Fax: (617) 497-6175

**Reflexite Corporation**
120 Darlington Drive
Avon, CT 06001-4217
(860) 676 7100
Fax: (860) 676 7199

**Russell Athletic**
755 Lee Street, PO Box 272
Alexander City, AL 35011-0272
(205) 329-4000
Fax: (205) 329-5308

**Schoeller Textil, USA Inc.**
2400 West Lake Avenue North
Suite 4
Seattle, WA 98109
(206) 283-6991
Fax: (206) 283-0703

**Solutia, Inc.**
1460 Broadway
New York, NY 10036
(212) 382-9600
Fax: (212) 382-9611

**Somitex Prints of California, Inc.**
17355 Railroad Street
City of Industry, CA 91748
(626) 965-8411
Fax: (626) 810-8247

**Sterling Fibers**
111 West 40th Street
New York, NY 10018
(212) 840-7354
Fax: (212) 840-7440

**Summit Knitting Mills, Inc.**
1460 Broadway
New York, NY 10036-7306
(212) 719-3190
Fax: (212) 575-4726

**Teijin America, Inc.**
10 West 50th Street 20th Floor
New York, NY 10022
(212) 308-8744
Fax: (212) 308-8902

**Texollini, Inc.**
2575 El Presidio Street
Long Beach, CA 90810
(310) 537 3400
Fax: (310) 537 3500

**Thomaston Mills, Inc.**
115 East Main Street
Thomaston, GA 30286
(706) 647-7131
Fax: (706) 646-5068

**Toray Industries (America, Inc.)**
600 3rd Avenue, 5th Floor
New York, NY 10016
(212) 922-3700
Fax: (212) 972-4279

**Travis Textiles, Inc.**
469 7th Avenue
New York, NY 10018
(212) 268-6001
Fax: (212) 736-8839

**Trevira**
3 Park Avenue, 37th floor
New York, NY 10016
(212) 251-8000
Fax: (212) 251-8037

**TYR Sport, Inc.**
15391 Springdale Avenue
Huntington Beach, CA 92649
(714) 897-0799
Fax: (714) 373-0903

**Unitika America Corporation**
666 5th Avenue
New York, NY 10103
(212) 765-3760
Fax: (212) 765-3771

**W. L. Gore & Associates, Inc.**
PO Box 729
Elkton, MD 21922-0729
(410) 392-3500
Fax: (410) 392-3949

**Wellman, Inc.**
1133 Avenue of the Americas
34th Floor
New York, NY 10036
(212) 642-0740
Fax: (212) 642-0759

**Wickers Sportswear, Inc.**
340 Veterans Memorial Highway
Commack, NY 11725
(516) 543-1700
Fax: (516) 543-1378

**Yarrington Mills Corp.**
412 South Warminster Road
Hatboro, PA 19040-0397
(215) 674-5125
Fax: (215) 674-0586

# GETTING
# IT ON

# GETTING
# IT ON

## ALL TRADEMARKED
## PRODUCTS AND THEIR
## SUGGESTED USES

179

# GETTING IT ON
## ALL TRADEMARKED PRODUCTS LISTED AND THEIR SUGGESTED USES

## INSULATION:

**ACTIVIST**
Tops, tights, bibs, full suits, pants, balaclavas

**adidas EQT TRI-QUILT**
Performance outerwear, tops and pants

**ARCTIC FLEECE**
Outerwear, outdoor wear, skiwear

**BERBER BY GLENOIT**
Mid to outer layer outdoor sportswear, outerwear.

**CHINELLA**
Outerwear, outdoor wear, skiwear

**CHINELLA LITE**
Outerwear, outdoor wear, skiwear, linings

**CITIFLEECE**
Sportswear, warm-ups

**CLOUD 9 FLEECE**
Warm-ups, active wear, leisure wear

**DENSIFIED BATTING**
Jackets, vests, bibs, quilted apparel & linings

**DYERSBURG E.C.O.**
Outerwear, sportswear

**DYERSBURG E.C.O. LITE**
Outerwear, sportswear

**DYERSBURG E.C.O. WOOL**
Outerwear, sportswear

**ECOPILE**
Active outerwear

**ECOPILE II**
Active outerwear

**ECO THERM**
Performance outerwear, headwear, hand-wear

**GLENAURA**
Outdoor sportswear and outerwear

**GLENPILE**
Outdoor sportswear and outerwear

**HIGHLANDER**
Light activewear, athleisure

**HIGHLANDER PLUS**
Light activewear, athleisure

**HOLLOFIL**
Outerwear, jackets, vests

**HOLLOFIL II**
Outerwear, jackets, vests

**KINDERFLEECE**
Outerwear, playwear, sportswear, kidswear

**LIFA ARCTIC**
Body garments, skating, biking

**MICROART**
Outdoor, ski, snowboarding

**MICRO-LOFT**
Outerwear, jackets, coats, bibs, gloves

**MICROPLUSH**
Sportswear, outerwear, accessories

**N/SL8**
Outerwear, sportswear

**NEOPRENE**
Scuba diving, surfing, skiing

**NORDIC SPIRIT**
Outerwear

**NUBLEND**
Warm-ups, jogging, aerobics

**OUTLAST**
Outerwear, linings, skiwear, climbing

**POLARGUARD 3D**
High performance outerwear, vests, jackets

**POLARGUARD HV**
High performance outerwear, vests, jackets

**POLARTEC 100 SERIES**
Performance apparel, expedition weight underwear, accessories, etc.

**POLARTEC 100 BIPOLAR**
Underwear, biking jerseys, performance shirts (next to the skin)

# GETTING IT ON

## ALL TRADEMARKED PRODUCTS LISTED AND THEIR SUGGESTED USES

**POLARTEC 200 SERIES**
Performance apparel, jackets, pullovers, pants, vests, shorts, etc.

**POLARTEC 200 BIPOLAR**
Performance apparel, jackets, pants, pullovers, (mid or outer layers)

**POLARTEC 300 SERIES**
Performance apparel, jackets, pants, pullovers, (mid or outer layers)

**POLARTEC 300 BIPOLAR**
Performance apparel, jackets, pants, pullovers, (mid or outer layers

**POLARTEC MICRO SERIES**
Performance shirting & apparel, cross-overwear (next to the skin)

**POLARTEC THERMAL STRETCH**
Performance apparel, tops, vests, tights, bras, shorts, (next to the skin) expedition

**PRIMALOFT**
Performance outerwear, head wear & hand-wear

**PROPILE**
Outdoor sportswear, outerwear

**QUALLOFIL**
Outerwear, jackets, vests

**REPLEX**
Tennis, golf, biking, athletic wear

**REPLEX LITE**
Tennis, golf, biking, athletic wear

**SNO-TEC**
Skiing, snowboarding, winter wear

**THERMA F.I.T.**
Running, hiking, snowboarding, cycling, etc.

**THERMA FLEECE**
Winter active, running, cycling

**THERMOLITE**
Outerwear, jackets, vests, bibs, footwear

**THERMOLOFT**
Outerwear, jackets, coats, bibs, gloves

**THINSULATE**
Apparel, gloves, footwear, skiwear, hunting

**THINSULITE LITE LOFT**
Apparel, gloves, footwear, etc.

**THINSULATE ULTRA INSULATION**
Apparel, gloves, footwear, etc.

**WORSTERLON**
Hunting gear, athleisure, etc.

**YUKON 2000**
High performance outerwear, vests, jackets

**YUKON FLEECE**
Performance activewear

**YUKON PROTEC**
Performance outerwear and sports-wear

## MOISTURE MANAGEMENT

**AKWADYNE**
Sportswear, intimate apparel, shell fabrics, fleeces

**AKWATEK**
Sportswear, intimate apparel, shell fabrics, fleeces

**BAGDAD**
Shorts, shirts, technical sports apparel

**BIO DRI**
Aerobics, biking, jogging, skating, athletics

**BREATHABLES**
Leotards, underwear, hosiery, bodywear

**CAMBRELLE**
Shoes

**CAPILENE**
Technical underwear, lining, insulation, socks

# GETTING IT ON

## ALL TRADEMARKED PRODUCTS LISTED AND THEIR SUGGESTED USES

**CMC**
Tops, tees, cover-ups, walking, running, biking, weight training, etc.

**COMFORTEX**
Biking, intimate apparel, sports bras, etc.

**COTTONWIQUE**
Medium weight outer shell fabric or inner

**DRICIIME**
Garment linings, long underwear

**DRI F.I.T.**
Running, tennis, golf, training, cycling, skiing, etc.

**DRILAYER**
First layer or outer garment

**DRI-LEX**
Shoes, fleece

**DRI-LEX AEROSPACER**
Shoes

**DRI-LEX FLEECE**
Shoes

**DRYLINE**
Running gear and other performance outerwear

**DRYLINER**
Fitness & sport bras

**DRYSPORT**
Cycling shorts, bibs, mountain biking

**DRYWICK**
Shirts, tops, action wear

**FIELDSENSOR**
Bikewear, linings

**HYDRASUEDE**
Fitness shorts, sports bras, running tights, cycling shorts, volleyball

**HYDROMOVE**
Running gear, cross training, fitness, soccer, basketball, tennis, cycling

**INTERA**
Performance activewear of all sorts

**LIFA ACTIVE**
Underwear

**LIFA ATHLETIC**
Body garments, skating, biking, etc.

**LOOPKNIT**
Outerwear, sportswear

**M.C.S.**
Technical sportswear, travel wear, adventure gear

**MAX**
Cycling, golf, shell lining

**NATUREXX**
Activewear, team sport, athletic wear, compression

**PHIN-TECH**
Underwear, linings

**POLARTEC100 SERIES BI-POLAR**
Underwear, bike jerseys, performance shirting

**QUICKWICK**
Team uniforms, swimwear, fleece garments, mountain biking, activewear

**RADIATOR**
Warm-ups, team sports, jogging, aerobics

**REACT**
Athletic shoes

**SCHOELLER dryskin**
Intensive sports, cross country skiing, hiking,

**SCHOELLER dynamic**
Climbing pants, mountaineering/ guide apparel, downhill ski suits backpacking, golf, tennis

**SYNCHILLA**
Outerwear, tops, jackets, vests

**T3 TACTEL AQUATOR**
Technical sportswear, tops, sport bras

**TACTEL AQUATOR**
Active wear, intimates, underwear, golf

# GETTING IT ON
## ALL TRADEMARKED PRODUCTS LISTED AND THEIR SUGGESTED USES

**ULTRASENSOR**
Aerobic sports, cycling, running

**WINNING COMFORT**
Cycling, running, wear, underwear, soccer

**YUKON LIGHTS**
Underwear, light weight performance wear

## WATERPROOF, WINDPROOF BUT BREATHABLE

**ACTIVENT**
Running, cycling, skiing, mountain biking, back packing

**amFIB**
Rainwear, cycling, running, foul weathergear

**AQUAGUARD**
Active wear

**BURLINGTON COMPOSITE TECH.**
Golf, snowboarding, technical outerwear

**CALTECH**
Outdoor rugged sportswear

**CANARI THERMO FLEECE**
Outerwear, skiwear

**CLIMA F.I.T.**
Running, cycling, skiing, golf, training

**CLIMAGUARD**
Light active wear, athleisure, shell fabrics

**COMFORTMAX IB**
Bibs, parkas, coats, pants, legwear, hats, gloves

**COMFORTMAX STRETCH**
Bibs, parkas, coats, pants, legwear, hats, gloves

**DARLEXX**
Athletic wear, ski wear, diving, water sports

**DERMIZAX**
Mountaineering, snowboarding, active wear

**DERMOFLEX**
Skiing, snowboarding

**DESTINY**
Shorts, jackets, rainwear, outerwear

**DRYLOFT**
Sleeping bags, baffled/quilted parkas

**DUREPEL**
Wind shirts, outerwear, skiing, snowboarding

**ENTRANT GII**
Activewear, mountaineering, skiing, snowboarding, trekking, bike wear

**EPICAL**
Performance outerwear

**EXOSKIN**
Water sports, apparel, headwear

**FILA TECH**
Wind wear, jackets, pants, warm ups, aerobics

**GORE-TEX**
Backpacking, camping, skiing, running, hunting, motor sport, fishing, outerwear

**GORE-TEX IMMMERSION**
Fishing waders, dry tops & dry suits for kayaking

**GORE-TEX OCEAN TECH.**
Off shore & coastal sailing gear

**GORE WINDSTOPPER**
Golf, shooting sports, hunting, backpacking, cycling, skiing, motorsport, outerwear

**H$_2$NO PLUS**
Ski jackets, ski pants, ski suits

**H$_2$NO STORM**
Ski jackets, ski pants, ski pants, shells

**H$_2$OFF**
Tennis, biking, skiing, trekking, activewear

# GETTING IT ON
## ALL TRADEMARKED PRODUCTS LISTED AND THEIR SUGGESTED USES

**HELLY TECH CLASSIC**
Outerwear, skiing, biking, fishing, camping hunting

**HELLY TECH LIGHTNING**
Outerwear, skiing, biking, fishing, camping hunting

**HELLY TECH PRO**
Outerwear, skiing, biking, fishing, camping

**HYDROFLEX**
Camping, skiing, snowboarding, hunting

**HYDRO THANE**
Jackets (polyester/cotton base cloths)

**HYDRO VINYL**
Jackets, bags, tarps, tents

**K-KOTE**
Outerwear, rainwear

**KLAY-KOTE**
Outerwear, rainwear

**MARMOT MEMBRAIN**
Outdoor apparel, tents

**MICROFT CONDENIER**
Skiwear, golf

**P.E.F.**
Pullovers, gloves, jackets, hats

**PERMIA**
Performance outerwear

**PNEUMATIC**
Shell fabrics, jackets, pants

**POLARTEC WINDBLOC**
Outerwear, jackets, vests, accessories

**PROOF ACE**
Outdoor sports, mountaineering, marine clothing

**SCHOELLER SKIFANS**
Climbing, skiing, trekking, snowboarding, performance outerwear

**SCHOELLER - WB FORMULA**
Mountaineering, skiing, snowboarding, trekking, biking

**SCHOELLER stretchlite**
Climbing, mountain biking, trekking, hiking, golf, tennis, pants, bibs, athleisure

**SKINFIT**
Competitive swimwear, active sports, performance wear

**STORMBREAKER**
Foul weather gear, dry suits, sailing, biking, camping, climbing, etc.

**STORM F.I.T.**
Running, outdoor sports, hiking, snow boarding

**STORM-TECH**
Outerwear snow boarding, etc.

**SUPER MICROFT**
Activewear, outerwear

**SYMPATEX**
Outerwear, knitwear, footwear, gloves, hats, horse blankets, etc.

**SYMPATEX WINDLINER**
Sweaters, fleece apparel, golf, etc.

**TORAYDELFY 2000**
Performance outerwear

**TRIAD**
Outerwear, medical garments, outdoor accessories

**TRIPHIBIAN**
Running & cycling tights, walking gear, mountain biking, all-weather exercise, etc.

**TRIPLE POINT CERAMIC**
Outerwear

**ULTRAMANIAC**
Running & cycling jackets, mountain biking, etc.

**ULTREX**
Snowboarding, skiing, outerwear, golf

**VAPEX**
Performance outerwear, headwear, gloves

**VERSATEC**
Bike jackets, wind shirts, outerwear

# GETTING IT ON
## ALL TRADEMARKED PRODUCTS LISTED AND THEIR SUGGESTED USES

**WHIRL WIND**
Cycling, golf, skiing, hiking

**WINDBRAKE**
Fleece jackets, sweatshirts, sweaters

## STRETCH

**COMPREXX**
Athletic wear, team sport, repetitive sports

**DARLEXX SUPERSKIN**
Speed shorts, luge, swimwear

**DARLEXX THERMALASTIC**
Ski tights, jackets, warm water diving

**E.C.T.**
Compression garments, tights, sports medicine

**ESP**
Active apparel, swimwear, jeans, cycling, wear, tights, leotards, other bottom weights

**FITNESS SLIMMERS**
Aerobic wear, dancewear, exercise, bodywear

**MCT**
Sports bras, running gear, aerobics, fitness training

**POLARTEC POWERSTRETCH**
Perfomance apparel, tops, vests, tights, bras, shorts

**REPLAY**
Cycling, running

**SPANDURA**
Rugged outerwear, climbing, swimwear, hunting, cycling, skiwear

**SPANDURA II**
Rugged outerwear, climbing, swimwear, hunting, cycling, skiwear

**SPANDURA FLEX-TEX**
Rock climbing, pants, rollerblading, mountain biking

**SUPERLOC**
Compression shorts, swimwear, tights

**SYNSATION**
Swimwear, aerobics, bodywear

## SPECIAL FABRICS

**AZUREAN**
Beachwear, boating gear, outdoor wear, shirts, tops, golf

**COVILLE'S MICROSTOP**
Performance wear

**DAZZLE FABRIC**
Team uniforms

**DIAMONDBACK**
Team sport, soccer, football

**DURAKNIT**
Team sport, athletic uniforms, trims

**EXPEL**
Shell fabrics, outerwear

**FILA 5**
Wind jackets & pants

**HYDRO FLAME**
Jackets, tents (nylon, polyester & cotton basecloths)

**illumiNITE**
Jackets, vests, shorts, caps, tee shirts

**inSIGHT**
Running, cycling, shorts, vests, jackets, tees, accessories

**LYCRA POWER**
Compression garments, bikewear, tights, sports medicine

**MICRO MESH**
Team sport jackets

**MICROTEP-25**
Competition swimming

**NU BLEND**
Warm ups, exercise gear, jogging

**PRO-BRITE**
Team sport, sports uniforms

**REACT**
Athletic shoe linings

**RHINO CLOTH**
Shoes & boots

# GETTING IT ON

## ALL TRADEMARKED PRODUCTS LISTED AND THEIR SUGGESTED USES

**SATIN PRO MESH**
Team sports, athletic uniforms

**SCHOELLER dynatec**
Snowboarding, motorcycle, hiking, outerwear

**SCHOELLER keprotec**
Cross-country & downhill skiing, mountain biking, cycling, snowboarding, motorcycling

**SCHOELLER keprotec with INOX**
Boots, skiwear, climbing, mountain biking, motorcycling, rugged outdoor wear

**SILENZZ**
Outerwear, hunting gear

**SKIN FIT**
Swim wear, cycling, aerobics, fitness

**SPECTRA/SOLUTION 7**
Rugged apparel, backpacks, luggage

**STUNNER**
Hiking, beachwear, tennis, golf, casual wear

**STUNNER QD**
Light exercise, jogging, tops

**TACKLE II/GUARDIAN**
Snowmobile suits, flotation gear

**TEFLON**
Outerwear, sportswear

**TIDAL WAVE**
Surfing, skiing, snowboarding, hiking, jackets

**TOUGHTEK**
Whitewater rafting pants, tough clothing, glove palms, slipper bottoms

**VIPER CLOTH**
Boots

**VISA**
Team apparel, activewear, athleisure

# GLOSSARY
# OF TERMS

# GLOSSARY OF TERMS

## ABRASION RESISTANCE:

A fabric's ability to hold up to the destructive action of rubbing. Abrasion causes a loss of appearance through fuzzing or pilling, erosion or destruction of insulating pile surfaces, or wear-through of the fabric itself in critical high abrasion areas. Example: elbows, knees, inner thigh areas, underarms, etc.

## ABSORPTION:

The attraction and retention of liquids or gases WITHIN the pores of a fiber or the retention of moisture between fibers, within yarns, and between fibers or yarns. Generally, this is the moisture management characteristic and mechanism of natural fibers and some synthetics.

## ADSORPTION:

The adhesion of an extremely thin layer of gas molecules and/or liquids to the solid surfaces of fibers within yarn structures, and between fibers or yarns within fabrics. There is very little, if any, penetration of gases or liquids into the fibers themselves but rather a movement of fluid along and around the fibers. Generally, this is the characteristic and mechanism of moisture management in synthetic fibers. (See Wicking)

## AIR PERMEABILITY:

The degree to which air is able to pass through a fabric, either entering or exiting the fabric. This is not equivalent to breathability.

## AIR-JET TEXTURING OR FLUID TEXTURING:

This is a continuous filament yarn texturing system that uses a high intensity stream of air (or steam) to blow across a relaxed yarn to separate the strands and form loops in the filaments. The strands become entangled and form a yarn with a high bulk but no stretch. Used frequently to produce textured nylon and polypropylene carpet yarns, sometimes called "BCF" (Bulked Continuous Filament) yarns.

## ANTI - MICROBIAL FINISHES AND YARNS:

Special treatments of fibers or fabrics to make them resist or retard the growth of biological organisms such as bacteria that can cause odor, skin irritation, fabric degradation, etc. Some treatments are both anti-microbial and anti-fungal, also giving protection from fungus, mildew and other odor and rot-causing organisms. In some cases, synthetic fibers are made with these chemical agents included with the polymer during extrusion and are considered to be inherent properties of those fibers, or actually part of the fiber itself, not added later like a finish. Such treatments tend to be more durable and long-lasting in effect.

## ANTI-STATIC FINISHES:

Finishes applied primarily to synthetic fibers that tend to develop static charges. These finishes dissi-

191

GLOSSARY OF TERMS

# GLOSSARY OF TERMS

pate electrical charges that build up on the fibers and thereby reduce static cling and the "zapping" that can take place when the wearer touches the door knob or other grounded surfaces.

## ARAMID FIBERS:

One of the second generation fibers available today for very high performance applications, aramid fibers are five times stronger than steel, weight for weight. Sold under the trademarks Kevlar® and Nomex® from DuPont and Trevar® from Hoechst Fibers, these fibers are used in materials and apparel that demand great strength and very little stretch or elongation. (example: bullet-proof vests, cut resistant gloves, competitive racing sails, industrial grade clothing, etc.) However, occasionally, these fibers find their way into performance fabrics to add extra wear, abrasion and tearing resistance.

## ATHLEISURE:

A casual term that describes garments that are designed to look like serious performance clothing (may contain authentic performance fibers, fabrics and finishes) but are actually intended to be worn as casual sportswear. "apres ski" clothing is a good example, designed to look like working skiwear, but lighter in weight and looser in fit.

## BACKING:

An extra amount of yarn or fabric added to, or attached to (knitted or woven in, quilted, bonded, laminated, etc.) a fabric to give it extra strength, support, opacity, thickness, weight or insulation.

## BLENDED YARNS:

Yarn in fabrics that are made up of two or more fiber types for the purpose of durability, performance, aesthetics, or cost. Tri-Blends are the blending of three fibers into one yarn for the purpose of performance, comfort (by the addition of an absorbent fiber in the mix), or for special cross-dyed color effects.

## BREATHABILITY:

The ability of a fabric to allow water vapor and excess heat to pass through and/or around the fibers and fabric construction or through pores and/or gaps in specially designed special films, membranes or coatings, allowing for more efficient evaporation of perspiration and heat generated by the body. This is not equivalent to permeability or wicking.

## BRIGHTNESS:

The degree to which light reflects off a fabric or yarn surface, resulting in increased clarity of colors, and shininess or gloss to the fabric's appearance. Brightness in a fabric can be affected by the fiber cross section, whether the fibers have

# GLOSSARY OF TERMS

delustering additives (causing them to take on a chalk-like appearance), the surface character of the fabric construction (example: a satin construction), a coating or other surface modification, like calendering, embossing or polishing. (See Cross section, Calendering and Coating)

## BRUSHED:

A fabric surface modification technique where special equipment raises the surface yarns or actually breaks, the surface fibers to make them fuzzy, or to create a plush surface as in the inside of warm-ups. This usually enhances their insulation value (by helping them trap body heat), appearance or "hand". This technique can be used on natural as well as synthetic fabrics. This is not to be confused with pile fabrics where special or extra yarns are added to the fabric construction to create a totally different type of surface. (See Pile and Sliver)

## CALENDERING:

A finishing process that imparts a flat, glossy, smooth surface to a fabric accomplished by passing the fabric between two super-heated rolls under enormous pressure. This is done to flatten and spread out the surface yarns, to close up the tiny gaps in the weave or knit, and/or to improve its resistance to wind or moisture. Also, the process increases the brightness and luster of a fabric, especially those fabrics made of synthetic fibers that

can be heat-set permanently in this flattened condition. If one or both of the rolls are engraved with a boldly definitive pattern, and the fabric is made from thermoplastic fibers or treated with heat-curable resins, the resulting effect is a transfer of the pattern profile to the fabric surface. This process is called **embossing**.

## CAPILLARY ACTION:

This is the process by which liquid moves through the pores of a fabric through adhesion and cohesion of the liquid to the fibers and fabric structure. The speed of movement depends on the surface tension of the liquid. (A good example is the movement of coffee percolating up a sugar cube when only the bottom edge of the cube touches the coffee surface. Try it!) This is the action that takes place in wicking or "push-pull" moisture management, or in the movement of perspiration through a fabric or material for evaporation in activewear. (See Wicking and Absorbency)

## CERAMIC WATERPROOF/ BREATHABLE COATING:

The technique of applying micro-fine silicon ceramic (silicon dioxide) particles to a polyurethane coating. This process is said to create two different sized pores in the micro-porous coating. In addition to the fine micro-pores normally created in the polyurethane coating application, pores that are more than five times smaller are also created where the ceramic particles and the polyurethane resin bond together. These extremely fine pores are reputed to be large enough, when combined with the normal micro-pore structure, to increase the fabric's **M.V.T.R.** (**M**oisture **V**apor **T**ransmission **R**ate), and add durability to the coating without decreasing the waterproofness.

## CHITIN COATING:

A coating developed in Japan made from crab shells which is sometimes applied to naturally hydrophobic fibers or fabrics to add water absorbency.

## CIRÉ:

A very bright, patent-leather-looking, shiny face or finish on a non-satin knitted or woven fabric. This effect is produced by applying wax to the fabric face with heat and pressure or, more commonly, by bonding a bright polymer film or applying a special resin or filler to the fabric and polishing it with enormous pressure, friction and heat. Aside from added water resistance, a ciré finish is purely an aesthetic fashion look.

## CLO OR CLO FACTOR:

"Clo" is a measurement of heat retention (or insulation value) in textiles and apparel. It is similar to the "R" Factor in home insulation,

but takes into account the variables of fabric and clothing constructions, and to a degree, human activity and movement. The Clo warmth evaluation system was developed by the Navy to test and evaluate high altitude flying suits prior to World War II. The testing of Clo is done with a guarded, heated plate over which a material (fabric) is positioned. The difference between the temperature under the fabric and above it determines the insulation value of the material or fabric. A special formula is then used to determine the Clo Factor of the fabric. The higher the number, the warmer the fabric.

## COATING:

A finishing process where a substance is spread or sprayed very thinly and evenly on one or on both sides of a fabric and permanently bonded to the fabric by chemistry, heat or both. When applied to the exposed face of the fabric, this is called FACE COATING. When applied to the back, it's called BACK COATING. Substances commonly used are vinyls, urethanes, acrylic and rubber latex, silicones, cellulose, sheeted rubber alone or with fillers. The result is designed to enhance the fabric's strength, appearance or luster, hand, water resistance, breathability (with water resistance), windproof performance (air permeability), reflectivity (see

# GLOSSARY OF TERMS

Metalizing and Reflectance), heat retention, flame resistance or weight. (See Windproof, Waterproof, Vapor Barrier, etc.)

## COLORFASTNESS:

The ability of a fabric to retain its color intensity and integrity when exposed to the elements such as laundering and dry cleaning, bleaching or exposure to chlorine-containing pool water, sunlight and/or other atmospheric pollutants. Colorfast performance depends upon the combination of fibers used in the fabric, dyestuffs and the dyeing method, the types of finishing after-treatments, as well as the time that the fabric is exposed to the degrading elements. The most colorfast fibers are those that have the color added to the synthetic fibers when they are made. These are called solution-dyed or dope-dyed fibers. Today, polypropylene fibers are the most common fibers to be created this way simply because they are so smooth, inert, and not dyeable that color cannot be added to them in any other way.

## COMFORT FINISHES:

Special topical finishes applied to hydrophobic fibers (predominately polyester) that make them hydrophilic, allowing the fabric to wick away perspiration from the skin. The wearer feels more comfortable, not like being wrapped in a plastic sheet. (See Wickable, Hydrophilic.)

## COMPRESSION FABRICS:

Specially designed elastic fabrics, usually made from synthetic fibers containing higher percentages of heavier denier spandex fibers that give them a lot of power stretch and recovery (modulus) in both length and width directions. Combinations of knit structures and Neoprene® foam rubber also can be considered in the same category and for the same uses. The purpose of these fabrics is to provide maximum support to the muscles in stressful and repetitive actions where the muscles tend to vibrate and move around unnecessarily, causing fatigue. It is claimed that compression fabrics used in properly designed garments can improve an athlete's performance by as much as 12% or more.

## CONDUCTION:

The transfer of body heat through a fabric by contact with another material or medium, such as air, snow, water, etc. Heat always flows from warm to cold; therefore, one of the methods of maintaining body warmth is controlling direct conduction of heat to the outside of a garment by layering, insulation, windproof barriers, coatings, laminated materials, etc. (See Convection, Radiation)

# GLOSSARY OF TERMS

## CONVECTION:

The movement and flow of warm air in relation to cold air. Warm air is lighter and rises while cold air is heavy and sinks. This process causes a constant air flow around the body that, if uncontrolled, can contribute to the loss of body heat through the head, the neck of a garment, from open sleeves or waist areas of a garment or though open pant legs. Therefore, garment construction using hoods, close fitting collars, elastic cuffs and waistbands, etc., as well as hats or caps, and gloves are all strategies to control convection heat loss. (See Conduction, Radiation)

## CORE SPUN YARNS:

Yarns that are made from a core fiber that is covered with another fiber (either continuous filament or spun) using a spinning or wrapping process for the purposes of aesthetics, strength, dyeability or stretch. The core fiber travels through a hollow spindle and is covered with another covering yarn when it emerges from the bottom. The process is used to create covered elastic or spandex fibers for fabric or hosiery applications. Special high bulk spun fibers are sometimes spun around a continuous filament nylon or polyester core for strength. There are even special, low twist cotton fabrics that use water-soluble covering fibers for strength in weaving or knitting which later dissolve in dyeing and finishing leaving behind loose, low twist, super-soft cotton yarns on fabric surface.

## CROSS SECTION:

The profile of the cut end of a fiber when viewed head on. All fibers, natural and synthetic, have specific cross sections, but only the synthetic fiber cross sections are determined by the shape of the hole drilled in the spinneret (extrusion head) during extrusion or manufacturing. (See Spinneret and Extrusion.)

In the case of cotton, its cross section looks like a collapsed drinking straw with a hollow core called the lumen in the middle. This hollow core is where water or perspiration moves through the fiber and is controlled after the fiber absorbs it. The wool fiber has a spongy core, called the medulla, that serves the same purpose as the lumen in cotton. Silk has a triangular cross section that contributes to its luster and brightness, etc. In synthetic fibers, the most common cross section is round, but a popular cross section is trilobal (having three facets or lobes). Pentalobal cross sections (five sides) are readably available as well. These specialized cross sections add or decrease the luster and light reflectance of the yarns as well as modify the hand or feel, and cleanability of the fabrics made from them.

# GLOSSARY OF TERMS

## CUT PROOF:

Super strong fibers such as Kevlar® and Spectra® will produce fabrics that offer great resistance to being cut with sharp objects. These fibers find utility in protective clothing applications where protection from knives and other sharp objects is desired.

## DPF:

Literally, "**D**enier **P**er **F**ilament". This is the numbering system used to denote the size of the filaments in synthetic continuous filaments and staple yarns (weight in grams of 9000 meters of fiber filament). This is obtained by dividing the yarn denier by the number of filaments in the yarn. Example: The "dpf" of the filaments in a 100 denier nylon yarn containing 100 filaments would be 1 "dpf". If the 100 denier yarn contained only 50 filaments, the "dpf" of each filament would be 2, thereby twice as large. In the case of microfibers, each filament must always weigh LESS than 1 "dpf". (i.e., 100 denier, 150 filaments - or .67 "dpf". (See Denier)

## DEAD AIR SPACE:

The air space that exists within a fabric, among fiber filaments, or inside hollow fiber cross sections, between fabric layers or within garment structures. It can also be created by a system of layered or laminated fabrics that interfere with air circulation in and around the fiber or fabric structure, thus preventing the loss of body heat by conduction, and to a lesser degree, convection and radiation. More importantly, the air trapped in dead air space is gradually heated by the body. Insulation strategies in activewear clothing are mostly designed to create such spaces and to trap and hold as much of this warmth as possible in the most rigorous conditions of wind, snow, rain and cold.

## DENIER:

A direct yarn numbering system for expressing the size of synthetic continuous filament and synthetic staple yarns (weight, in grams, of 9,000 meters of yarn). The higher the denier index number, the heavier the yarn. This is opposite from the weight numbering system used in cotton count where the larger the weight index number, the finer and lighter the yarn. Example: 1/ 28=s, cotton count is heavier than 1/36=s. However, 40 denier nylon is much finer than 100 denier. (Also see Microdenier)

## DOWN:

The very fine, soft feathers found under the outer feathers of all types of water fowl, especially geese and ducks (classically, from eider ducks - ergo: eiderdown). Because of its extreme fineness and fluffy character, it can trap a

# GLOSSARY OF TERMS

great amount of body heat with little weight when used as an insulating layer in apparel and bedding and is among the most efficient (and expensive) insulating materials known.

## DOWNPROOF:

Fabric structures that resist the passage or poking-through of down feathers or other insulating materials used between the outer shell and lining fabrics.

## DRAPABILITY:

A term used to describe fabric softness and relates to the way a fabric hangs or falls in a relaxed state. The opposite is stiffness.

## D.W.R. FINISHES:

Literally, **D**urable **W**ater **R**epellent finishes. These finishes are water resistant chemicals applied and fixed to the shell fabric face, or some sort of coating applied and set into the fabric, or even an impervious membrane bonded to the fabric to repel water. In all cases, these applications are the first line of defense to keep rain from wetting-out and penetrating of the fabric. Some of these finishes, coatings and films are somewhat breathable, allowing water vapor (evaporated perspiration) to escape while keeping out the rain.

## ELASTANE:

Another generic term for spandex elastomeric (elastic-like) fiber.

## EXTRUSION:

The process of forming synthetic fiber by forcing a molten mass of fiber polymer (nylon, polyester, acrylic, olefin or polypropylene), or chemically dissolved cellulose (i.e., rayon, acetate, etc.) through a spinneret or small "shower head"-looking metal disc with minute holes drilled in it. The material that exits these tiny holes form endless continuous filaments that are dried or cooled and pulled together into a bundle of fibers that become a continuous multi-filament yarn. Some of these yarns are chopped up into short pieces or staple fibers to be spun into yarns by themselves, or are combined and blended in the spinning process with other natural or synthetic fibers to form blended spun yarns. Sometimes, two different types of synthetic polymers are extruded together for a specific purpose. As example, there are synthetic yarns that are made with two different polymers that shrink at different rates, resulting in a textured fabric after the fabric is relaxed and finished without pre-texturing the yarns first. (See Blended Fibers, Filament Yarn, Microdenier or Microfibers, Spun Yarns, etc.)

# GLOSSARY OF TERMS

## FABRIC WEIGHT:

Usually measured in ounces per linear or square yard, or gram per square meter. (Make sure you know which when seeking this information.) Keep in mind that the weight of a fabric has little, if anything, to do with how well it will insulate or how hard wearing it will be. Questions related to insulation value depend on the amount of the body's heat that can be trapped in the fabric's dead air space or reflected back to the body, not the weight of the fabric. Also, some of the strongest and most hard-wearing fibers and fabrics are synthetic and are among the lightest fibers in weight relative to many of the heavier natural fibers.

## FACE FINISHING:

The term used to describe fabrics that have been napped, sueded, embossed, or calendered. Fabrics are passed through appropriate machines that alter the feel or appearance of the fabric face.

## FIBER MIGRATION:

In the case of fiberfills or feather insulators used in apparel or bedding, there is a tendency for the fibers or feathers to gradually migrate through the lining or shell fabrics, causing skin irritation, "scratchiness" and general unsightliness in the appearance of the garment (pilling). The problem is commonly addressed by using very tightly woven or knitted shell or lining fabrics that are not penetrated by the insulating fibers or feathers. In the case of synthetic fiberfills, a non-woven scrim or web is sometimes placed between the fiberfill and the lining or shell fabrics, or is bonded to them. In other cases, the fiberfill material itself is designed so it doesn't penetrate the outer fabric structure and is termed "downproof."

## FILAMENT YARN:

An endless, continuous strand of fiber made from polymers (long chain molecules) using wet, dry or molten spinning systems equipped with spinnerets and made up of one or, usually, more filaments. Also, one of nature's own continuous filament yarns is silk produced by silkworms that have built-in spinnerets and create their own natural, organic polymers out of mulberry or oak leaves, spinning them into cocoons as one continuous strand or filament. The spider does a pretty good job of producing another type of continuous filament silk to catch lunch and dinner. (See Spinneret)

## FILLING OR WEFT OR WOOF:

In a woven structure, the yarns that run across the width of a fabric from selvage to selvage at 90 degrees to the lengthwise yarns

GLOSSARY OF TERMS

are called weft yarns. The length-wise yarns are call the woof. Weft yarns are also called filling or "picks" while woof is also called warp or "ends". In fabric analysis, the number of picks and ends per inch or centimeter is used to designate the fabric construction and is an indication of the fabric's fineness and weight. Weft is also referred to in circular knitting whereby the yarns are knitted in a horizontal or weft direction. As a result, circular knitting is sometimes called weft knitting.

## FLAME RETARDANT:

The term used to describe fabrics that do not continue to burn when the ignition source is removed from contact. Flame retardant chemicals may be added as finishes, into the coatings or may be included with the synthetic polymer at the time the fiber is extruded. Some fibers are inherently flame retardant (Nomex®, Kevlar®, etc.) This is an important quality for protective clothing for firefighters.

## FLUORO-POLYMER:

The synthetic polymer created by DuPont that is marketed under the Teflon® trademark. It is better known in the performance activewear industry as the base component for the GoreTex®- type permeable (water resistant but breathable) membrane. Another chemical modification of fluoro-

polymers utilizing similar type chemistry is used as a fabric finish (DuPont's Teflon® Fabric Protector and 3M's Scotchgard®). It is a very effective, durable, liquid-borne stain protector for apparel and home furnishings.

## GARMENT DYEING:

The process of creating a garment from un-dyed fabric and applying the color to the garment after it has been assembled, as opposed to dyeing the fabric first, or dyeing the yarns before knitting or weaving them into fabric, and then creating the garment. There is good news and there is bad news - Good news! Garments may be made in bulk using un-dyed fabric (prepared for garment dyeing by scouring and/or pre-shrinking) and kept on the shelf until the customer selects the desired color. Then the garment is placed in a dye bath and the whole garment is dyed at once. This eliminates the inventory of pre-colored fabric and allows a very fast turnaround for the garment manufacturer by not having to wait for specially dyed fabrics. Bad news! Garments dyed in this manner must be over-sized in manufacturing to compensate for potential shrinkage, seams may pucker because of differential shrinkage between the fabric and the sewing thread, garments made from circular knitted fabrics may "torque" or develop a spiral shape

# GLOSSARY OF TERMS

distortion in dyeing, and all components of the garment must be made from the same fiber, otherwise color variations will occur. Other problems may exist and must be compensated for in manufacturing.

## HAND:

The illusive, subjective, aesthetic characteristic of a fabric or material determined by touch or "feel". "Hand" is made up of a combination of fabric texture, loft, bulk and body as perceived by an individual.

## HIGH LOFT:

Certain types of insulating products or materials that have large amounts of dead air spaces in the material or fiber structures and are designed to be resistant to "clumping", or matting in storage, care or wear.

## HYDROPHILIC:

Literally, "water loving". Fibers or fabrics that easily absorb and/or transport moisture in liquid form. It is possible to chemically treat hydrophobic (water hating) fibers and fabrics (usually synthetic fibers) to make them hydrophilic to one degree or another.

## HYDROPHOBIC:

Literally, "water hating". Fibers and fabrics that do not absorb liquid water at all or very slightly. This characteristic is common to most melt spun polymer-generated synthetic fibers, such as polypropylene, polyester and acrylic (nylon is fairly hydrophilic). However, many of these fibers, either by their nature or by chemical modification, can demonstrate various degrees of useful moisture management, such as wicking.

## INHERENT

(As In "Finish"): Literally, "as a part of ". Any property of a fiber, a yarn or a fabric that is built-in, engineered-in or is a natural, integral part of the product. This could be a special chemical added to the fiber or yarn structure during manufacture so as to become a part of the fiber or yarn itself. Commonly, some wicking, flame resistant and anti-microbial finishes are applied to synthetic fibers and yarns in this manner when the products are still in melt or formative state in order to give them "inherent" properties.

## INSULATION:

Any material, combination of materials or fabric systems that collect or maintain body heat, or reflect, or protect the body from external heat sources.

## KNITTED FABRICS:

Fabrics that are constructed from an interlocking series of yarn loops either created by hand or by machines. Knitted fabrics generally have a lot of stretch to them and

# GLOSSARY OF TERMS

many have two-way stretch (especially circular knits and flat bed knits as well as certain spandex-containing warp knits). They are easily moldable and body fitting and are generally very drapable and wrinkle resistant. In general, they tend to be looser in construction than wovens, and, although they readily trap air for superior insulation value, they are also more porous and receptive to air penetration, and perhaps, not the best choice for a "shell" or outer fabric where air or water penetration is undesirable (unless some type of filler, film or coating is applied to the knit to fill the holes). There are generally three major categories of knitted fabric constructions: flat bed (sweaters, fully fashioned knits, etc.), circular knits (jerseys, ribs, interlocks and double knits), and warp knits or tricot knits. Circular knits are by far the most common of all knits used in all apparel applications, including sporting goods apparel. However, warp knits are important in swimwear, compression fabrics, brushed linings, shell fabrics, lightweight running clothes and meshes, just to name a few applications.

## LAMINATION:

A technique used to bond or permanently link two or more fabrics and/or other layered materials together using adhesives, chemistry, or heat. This is done to enhance the performance over and above either material used alone. The resulting composite product must be considered as a "fabric system" as opposed to a fabric.

## LIGHTFASTNESS:

The term used to describe the degree to which a dyed fabric fades when exposed to sunlight. Lightfastness is mainly related to the dye selected to achieve the desired color. Some dyestuffs have considerably better lightfastness than others and it is up to the dyer to make proper selections.

## LYOCELL®:

A new, improved variant of cellulose-based apparel fibers developed by Courtaulds Fibers, Inc., U.K. and marketed internationally under the trademark, TENCEL®. The fiber is produced from wood pulp using a special solvent spinning process that allows the recovery and recycling of nearly all of the solvent, keeping the process envionmentally friendly. The resulting fiber has a wet and dry strength far superior to most other cellulose fibers, tends to retain its shape when wet and has an absorbency rate greater than cotton by weight. Easily dyeable and printable and with a good natural luster, **LYOCELL®** would make a comfortable and attractive apparel fabric.

# GLOSSARY OF TERMS

## M.V.T.R:

**M**oisture **V**apor **T**ransmission **R**ate or breathability. This term refers to the rate at which a fabric or permeable material will allow perspiration as water vapor to move from the inside to the outside of the material for evaporation, or to another medium for disposal. There are two major approaches to achieve this. One is for the vapor to mechanically pass through a hydrophobic (water hating) laminate, or a coating that contains thousands of micropores that are so fine that a raindrop cannot pass through. The other is a molecular or chemical type of monolithic (solid as opposed to micro-porous) hydrophilic (water loving) laminate or coating that absorbs the water molecules by breaking the surface tension of the water molecules and absorbing it through the membrane (a hydrophilic monolithic membrane).

## MEMBRANE:

An extremely thin film or coating that is usually laminated to a base fabric or between two or more fabrics to create a "barrier", usually to control water and wind penetration. Most commonly, the membranes used for performance activewear have microscopic pores built-in that are too small to admit water, snow, rain or moisture and most air flow, but large enough to allow for water vapor or excess heat to escape, creating the characteristic of "breathability".

## METALIZING:

The process of coating a fabric with a heat-reflecting metallic substance. One way to accomplish this is to take a metal-coated polymer film (covered with an extremely thin coating of metal) and bond it directly to the inside of a fabric which reflects the body's radiant heat back to keep the wearer warm. One problem is that the "metalized" film is noisy and rustles and can be stiff in cold conditions. In another technique, vapor deposits an aluminum coating onto the fiber in a fabric (usually made of polyester), resulting in a fabric that has each fiber covered with a bonded coating of metal. If done properly, the coating does not interfere with the softness or flexibility of the fabric. When used as an inner lining or laminated inside clothing, the metal coating reflects back the body's radiant heat, would otherwise be lost.

## MICROCRIMPED:

A process for imparting microscopic crimp, wrinkles or curls to a continuous filament or cut staple synthetic fiber using special fiber texturing technology and a heat-setting technique using the thermoplastic (heat-settable) character or the fibers to make the texture permanent. This gives the originally smooth synthetic fibers texture, bulk and/or stretch, improving the fiber's hand and insulating properties (creating more air spaces between the filaments of the yarn), as well as changing the appearance and stretch characteristics of the fiber and the fabrics.

## MICRODENIER OR MICROFIBERS:

Synthetic fibers (either continuous filament or staple) that have been extruded with extremely fine individual filaments that make up the total fiber bundle. Each filament must be less than one denier (the average fineness of cultured silk filaments) to be classified as a microfiber. The resulting yarns and fabrics are VERY soft to the touch and produce a "peach skin" or sueded feel and they are very easily brushed, napped or sueded. In addition, the very fine filament yarn bundles create more dead air spaces between them and have somewhat more insulating value for weight and bulk than non-micro fabrics. Also, because of their great coverage in the fabric structure, fabrics made from microfibers are claimed to be more water and wind resistant than ordinary fabrics made from non-micro fibers.

## microPCMs (Microencapsulated phase change materials)

Phase Change Materials (PCMs) that are chemically encased in a microscopic-sized shell material that is usually 150 microns or smaller in size. (The smallest water drop is 100 microns in size.) These are coated on a fabric or built into synthetic fibers when they are made and are used to create temperature regulation (warmth retention and heat control) in the fibers and fabrics they are applied to.

## MICROPOROUS:

Very tiny holes in a membrane, coating or film in a fabric system that allow breathability while resisting water penetration. To give an example of how fine these pores are, an average raindrop is 100 microns in size, while the pores in microporous membranes, films and coatings range anywhere from 0.1 to 10 microns in size. Such fine pores will not allow water (and virtually no wind) to penetrate the membrane; however, since the size of water vapor exists as 0.0004 microns in size, it can easily passes through the micropores, creating what is called breathability in a fabric.

# GLOSSARY OF TERMS

## MODULUS (YOUNG'S MODULUS)

Officially, "The ratio of change in stress to change in strain." It is the property of perfectly elastic materials (rubber, latex, spandex and some elastomeric films). Modulus is determined and calculated using various laboratory test methods and formulas. The resulting information indicates the "power" of the fabric or fiber to recover while under stress. As example, a fabric with a high modulus rating would have a lot of compression or "holding power," ideal for "power" activewear or for foundation apparel applications. Lower modulus fabrics might be better suited to comfort stretch or light control garments, such as swimwear, panties or fashion stretch applications.

## OIL REPELLENCY:

The measure used to describe a fabric's ability to resist oily stains. Fluorochemical finishes topically applied to fabrics not only renders them water repellent, but also oil repellent. These finishes impart the greatest measure of liquid stain resistance that is known today.

## OLEFIN, POLYPROPYLENE or POLYOLEFIN:

Olefin is the generic chemical term for the petroleum-based polypro-pylene fiber. The term polyolefin is another name for polypropylene (olefin). It is a VERY lightweight fiber and is the only commonly used fiber that has a specific gravity lighter than water; in fact, it floats when placed in water. Also, olefin has excellent wicking properties in spite of the fact that it is the most hydrophobic (water hating) fiber known. The fiber's excellent wicking property is caused by its extremely smooth, pore-less surface that offers no resistance to water's movement along and around the fiber through capillary action in wicking. Having no pores or openings on the fiber surface to hold dye molecules, it cannot be dyed or colored after it is extruded. Therefore, color must be added to the melted polymer before being extruded and solidified into yarn. This type of dyeing is called producer-dyed or solution-dyed and is the most colorfast of all dyeing methods.

## PERMEABILITY:

A fabric characteristic that allows moisture, air, or vapor to pass through it and its fibers or layers. The degree of permeability depends mainly upon the size of the holes, pores or gaps in the fabric, film or coating. As example, it is possible to have gaps or pores so small that water droplets and wind cannot penetrate, even under pressure, yet still allow water vapor to escape readily.

## PERSPIRATION FASTNESS:

The resistance of a dyed fabric to not lose or transfer color to another fabric when subjected to a solution simulating human perspiration. This test helps identify dyed fabrics that, because of improper treatment in or after dyeing, can cause staining when worn.

## PHASE CHANGE MATERIALS:

A material that will absorb or liberate large quantities of heat without an appreciable temperature change within it while changing state or phase. When contained in microscopic capsules (beads), this material can be applied to fibers or fabrics and used to create temperature regulating fibers or fabrics for warmth regulating systems.

## PIECE DYEING:

The most common way to dye fabric. The fabric is dyed after it has been woven or knitted. Sometimes the entire lot is handled as a single batch and other times the fabric moves through a series of non-stop processes that scour or clean the fabric, dye it, rinse it, and finish it. Finishes include softeners, water repellents or wicking finishes, etc. If the piece-dyed fabric is made

from thermoplastic fibers such as nylon or polyester, it may be just dried and heat set. This is the most economical way to dye and finish fabrics. (See Yarn Dyeing and Garment Dyeing.)

## PILE:

Raised fibers protruding from the fabric face, back or both which are formed by knitting or weaving in significant amounts of extra staple fiber to either or both sides of the fabric structure, brushing up, raising or napping the extra fibers and shearing (cutting) them to clean up the resulting "plush" or "pile" surface. The resulting fabric face(s) not only has a soft hand, it significantly increases the insulation value of the fabric as well as adding another dimension of cozy comfort. This type of fabric construction is also the source of most fake fur fabrics and fleeced knit goods used in sweat clothing.

## PILLING:

Pilling is formation of small balls or clusters of fibers that appear on the surface of fabrics and nearly always occur in garment areas of heavy wear and/or abrasion. All fibers pill but with weaker fibers such as natural and some cellulose-based synthetic fibers, the pills break or drop off and the fabric surface merely gets thinner at that spot . (Those "pills" are among the things your vacuum cleaner is

constantly picking up every day.) In general, synthetic fibers, such as acrylic, nylon, polypropylene and polyester, are so strong that the broken fibers or roughed up staples tend to hang on to each other and the strong fiber acts as an anchor preventing the pill from detaching from the surface. The accumulation of pills on fabrics stems from the pills being formed faster than they break off. The only real solution is to shave them off periodically. (Note: Today, there are new, high performance, low-pill acrylic and polyester fibers available that resist pilling. These fibers are weaker than the usual types so the anchor fibers are more easily broken, allowing the pills to shed.)

## PLY:

The combining of two or more single strands of yarn to form a larger, heavier yarn in order to add strength, bulk or even aesthetics to the resulting plied yarn. Also, the term "ply" can refer to the individual layers of laminated or layered fabrics.

## POLYMER:

A large molecule that is produced naturally or synthetically by linking together shorter molecules (monomers) in a chainlike structure. Manmade synthetic fibers are derived from polymers.

## POLYMERIZATION:

The conversion of monomers into much larger molecules (called polymers) through chemical reactions.

## POLYAMIDE:

The generic chemical name for the polymer also known as nylon. Commonly used in Europe in place of the term "nylon" to describe the fiber in a fabric. DuPont invented the process to make polyamide in the 1930's and gave it the trademark, "Nylon®". However, when the technology to make nylon moved to Europe, many European chemical companies tended to adopt the generic name polyamide, or developed their own marks for the fiber rather than use the DuPont mark. Later, the term "nylon" became so widely used in a casual manner that a court judged it to be a generic term and DuPont lost its exclusive copyright. Today, the term polyamide is still commonly used on European fabrics and garments made of nylon.

## PUSH-PULL:

In the process of evaporation, these two processes take place separately and at the same time. The "push" aspect of moisture transfer occurs when the body produces a lot of perspiration and the liquid and/or water vapor is literally "pushed" or pumped through and around the fabric structure from the inside to the outside for evaporation. The "pull" action is created by the rapid transfer of perspiration away from the body as evaporation takes place from the other side of the fabric, or by a readily absorbent outer layer of fibers or fabric that sucks up the moisture from the inner layer. In this case, the outer layer takes up the moisture faster than the inner layer and "pulls" it or moves it away from the body for evaporation.

The "push" effect also comes into play in the case of electrostatic (ionized) fabric treatments where the perspiration largely stays in vapor form as it moves through fibers and fabric. Using this method, supposedly direct contact of the skin to a moisture saturated fabric is not essential for the mechanism of the "push" effect to work (as in wicking) in the evaporation process. The electrically charged (ionized) fabric keeps the moisture mostly in vapor state that easily moves through the fibers and fabric to evaporate as fast or as slowly as the body generates perspiration.

## RADIATION:

The third way that the body regulates heat. (The other mechanisms are conduction and convection.) Radiant heat produced by the body travels easily through fabrics and clothing unless it is reflected back to the body. Usual insulating materials designed to trap body heat have little or no effect on this process. The radiant heat produced by the body is mostly lost continuously unless a reflective barrier is placed in its way, such as metalized or reflective material positioned between the body and the outer shell of the garment. (See Convection, Conduction and Metalizing)

## RECOVERY:

The ability of a fabric to return to its original shape and dimension after being stretched. This ability may be helped by the addition of bulked, stretch continuous filament fibers, spandex or natural rubber to the fabric structure.

## RETROREFLECTION:

Reflection in which the reflected rays of light are nearly totally sent back to their source. This means that a fabric or garment that is coated or treated with a substance that has this property, when it is hit by a projected light (headlights?), will throw back to the source nearly as much light as it receives with little, if any, scattering of light, thus, safely and clearly illuminating the wearer to the driver.

## SEAM SEALING:

The process of sealing all stitch lines and seams in a garment that is made from stormproof or waterproof fabric containing an

impervious, but breathable membrane, film or coating. This is to insure that no water penetrates the finished garment. Top-of-the-line companies require such processes be done and certified to before their trademarks are applied to the garments containing their fabrics. Commonly, heat sealing (welding) tapes or curable sealing glues are used for this purpose.

## SLIVER & SLIVER KNITTING:

Sliver is a loosely combined strand (bundle) of staple fibers that are all parallel to each other (usually about as big around as your thumb) that results from the carding, blending or combing operations in creating spun yarns. Sliver has no twist added at all, with only a slight "crimp" or pressed-in texture used to help hold the fibers together. Sliver knitting is a circular knitting process where the sliver is drawn in, knitted and tied in as a backing. The loose end of the sliver bundle forms a pile or a plush face to the fabric which is later napped and sheared to even out the pile face. These fabrics are used in performance outerwear, garment linings, warm-ups and other performance fabrics.

## SOIL RELEASE:

Oily soils and stains on fabrics made out of synthetic fibers are difficult to remove by laundering. Soil release finishes topically applied improve this undesirable feature. For example the same comfort finishes that make polyester fibers hydrophilic will also improve a textured fabric's ability to release oily stains when laundered.

## SPANDEX:

A special, stretchable, polyurethane elastomeric (rubber-like) synthetic fiber. It can stretch over 5 times its original length and fully recover to its original dimension immediately. Small percentages of spandex combined with other yarns are used to make hosiery, swimwear, foundation garments, actionwear fabrics, bodywear and other form-fitting apparel. Greater percentages of spandex are found in those garment applications that contain compression fabrics. Spandex is today's synthetic rubber fiber.

## SPECTRA® POLYETHELENE FIBER:

Produced by Allied Signal, this special polyethelene fiber rivals aramid fibers in strength and durability. Many times stronger than steel by weight, Spectra® fibers are used in a wide variety of end uses requiring great breaking strength, super hard wear, abrasion resistance and resistance to tearing and puncturing. This fiber can be found in the performance wear and accessories markets ranging from mountain climbing clothing and gear to backpacks and gloves.

## SPUN YARNS:

Yarns created from staple fibers (natural or synthetic) of similar lengths that are combined using one of several spinning process (i.e., ring spun, open-end or rotor spun, air jet spun, etc.). The staple fibers (pieces of fiber with relatively short lengths, such as cotton, wool, flax, etc.) are carefully cleaned, blended and carded into a parallel bundle (sliver) that are later drawn down to a desired size (diameter and weight) and twisted to hold them together, forming a continuous strand. These yarns are used in knitting, weaving or other fabric forming processes. Spun yarns tend to be "fuzzier" and "hairier" than continuous filament yarns. (See Blended Yarns) Occasionally, the paralleled fiber yarn bundles (sliver) are knit directly into pile or plush fabrics using special equipment.

## STAIN RESISTANCE:

Certain finishes will protect fabrics from liquid stains. For example, fabrics finished with fluoro-chemical finishes (Teflon® Fabric Protector, Scotchgard®) will resist being wetted by most liquid stains. Both water and oil borne stains will bead up and therefore can be blotted away before they soak into the fabric. Certain silicone finishes are effective against water borne stains but not oil borne stains.

## STAPLE FIBERS:

The term that describes the short fibers used to produce spun yarns. All natural fibers except silk (silk is a continuous filament fiber) occur in staple lengths. Synthetic fibers are first created as continuous filaments and must be cut up into specified lengths in order to be spun. The cut synthetic fibers are then called staple. If blending is to be done, the synthetic fiber must be cut into staple lengths that would be compatible with that of the intended blending partner fiber(s) in spinning.

## TEAR RESISTANCE:

The ability of a fabric to resist tearing, puncturing or abrasion failure. A fiber's and fabric's strength, density, tightness of construction and coatings can all contribute to this ability.

## TEXTURIZING:

The process of converting straight continuous filament yarns into bulkier yarns. In the texturizing process, the straight filaments develop permanent kinks and curls by heat-setting the texture into synthetic filament fibers such as nylon, polyester, polypropylene, etc. The texture can impart added bulk and springiness to the fibers, improve stretch and recovery, create a softer or harsher hand or "fluff-up" the yarn to create more air spaces between the filaments for better insulation. Texturing can also change the luster of the fiber, improve its wicking characteristics, increase the fiber's coverage capabilities and other properties not otherwise existing in the fiber before texturizing.

## THERMOPLASTIC:

The ability of melt spun fibers to be softened by the application of high heat and to allow themselves to be stretched, textured, molded or otherwise changed in dimension or shape and then to maintain that new shape or configuration when cooled. This allows fibers such as nylon and polyester (or fibers or fabrics containing them) to be heat set to prevent shrinkage, to permanently hold a crease, to be textured, to be polished or to be embossed.

## TOPICAL

(As In "Finish"): A finish or process that is applied to and locked in a fiber, yarn or fabric (usually to a fabric by some sort of "curing" or "fixing" process) after the product is constructed. Topical finishing processes can impart special performance characteristics to the product, such as water resistance (DWR finishes), wicking finishes, some anti-microbial finishes, etc. Topical finishes are applied to the surface of the product, or "topically".

## TRICOT:

A very wide knitted fabric made on a flat-bed tricot knitting machine. It is sometimes referred to as "warp knitted" because the fabric is created from the warp direction or lengthwise oriented yarns. The many ends of yarn are knitted together in the warp direction with thousands of needles set in a flat bed to form fabrics that are generally lightweight, strong and very stable in length but stretchy in width. By adding spandex fibers and by changing the construction, the fabrics can be made to have one or two-way stretch. Commonly used to produce swimwear, compression fabrics, foundation garments, lightweight running shorts, meshes, brushed lining, shell fabrics, and backing fabrics for quilting and laminates plus many more applications for performance apparel and accessories.

## TWO-WAY STRETCH:

Circular or warp knitted fabrics with spandex fibers that stretch in both length and width for maximum comfort and control. Although circular knitted fabrics tend to be two-way stretch fabrics anyway, the use of textured fibers or spandex somewhere in the fabric structure gives them more compressive "power" (modulus) and recovery.

# GLOSSARY OF TERMS

## VAPOR BARRIER:

A layer (coating, membrane, etc.) which totally prevents water vapor or air from passing through a fabric. Vapor barriers in activewear fabric design are intended to keep cold air and moisture out, and to keep the body's warmth and humidity inside a garment without inviting condensation and discomfort to the wearer.

## MOISTURE VAPOR TRANSMISSION:

The property of a material or fabric system to transmit water vapor through the material or fabric to the outside environment over a specified period of time, usually without allowing rainwater or outside moisture to penetrate the material. This system works on the principle of the "push" method of moisture management where the body's production of moisture as water vapor is enough to create an outward pressure on the fabric system that "pushes" the water vapor through the material to an outer layer of fabric or to the outside environment. The efficiency of fabric systems that allow vapor transmission is dependent upon several factors, not the least of which are the size of the "pores" or openings in the "permeable" or microporous membrane, film or coating.

## WPB:

Literally, **W**ater**p**roof and **B**reathable. A commonly used abbreviation to identify a wide variety of microporous, but hydrophobic (water hating) membranes or films laminated to other fabrics, or to applied coatings of polyvinyl chloride, polyurethane, ceramic or amino acid compounds that resist rain and wind penetration while allowing perspiration water vapor to escape. This is accomplished by creating thousands of micro-pores (5 -10 microns) that are far finer than the size of a raindrop (100 microns) but much larger than water vapor (0.0004 microns). This allows water vapor to escape while keeping raindrops from penetrating the WPB film, membrane or coating layer.

## WARP:

The set of yarns that run the length of a woven or warp knitted fabric. In woven fabrics, the warp makes up half of the fabric. The filling or weft yarns form the other half of the fabric and are interlaced perpendicular to the warp yarns from selvage to selvage. In denim fabrics, the warp yarns are pre-dyed while the filling or weft yarns remain white to give denim its distinctive look. Of the two, the warp yarns tend to be stronger and provide the foundation for the woven fabric structure while the styling yarns tend to be the filling

yarns. In warp knit fabrics, the entire fabric is formed by interlacing two or more adjacent warp yarns with a special knitting technique that needs no other filling yarn system to form a fabric.

## WATERPROOF:

Totally impervious to water penetration. Traditionally and even today, this is achieved through the use of some sort of coating, laminate, wax or other chemical substance that blocks all the tiny interstices or spaces in the fabric structure and yarns and fills in all the sites on a natural fiber that would normally allow for absorption of water. Through recent research and development, a whole, new generation of water hating (hydrophobic) membranes, films and coatings now exist that can totally block the penetration of moisture into a fabric structure, while allowing the body's moisture vapor to escape. Also, there are several new tightly constructed fabrics made with very fine micro-fiber filling yarns that are water and windproof without coatings, chemicals, membranes or films.

## WATER REPELLENCY:

A fabric's ability to shed water under most conditions. The water will bead up and not penetrate the fabric. This water shedding action is usually created by the application of a hydrophobic finish (either waxes, silicones or fluorochemicals). A well treated fabric will allow the user to come in from a rainshower, shake and remove almost all of the surface water from the garment. The less water that clings to the fabric, the better the water repellency.

## WATER RESISTANT:

The ability of a fabric to prevent liquid water from passing through. A very vague term that could mean anything from extremely water resistant to somewhat "fog-proof" and everything in between. Seek more definitive performance information if this is the only assurance of water or rain protection shown on a product.

## WICKING:

The ability of a fabric to move liquid water from one point to another through pores and channels within the fabric and fibers. The moisture moves rapidly along the channels formed by the fibers and yarns, helping it pass quickly through a fabric for moisture control and evaporation. This property can be built into a fiber such as polypropylene and polyester, or it can be enhanced by the use of certain chemical treatments either during the creation of the fiber or added topically in finishing after the fabric is made.

## WIND CHILL:

The amplified loss of body heat caused by the rapid movement of cold air and wind over a human or over the fabrics and garments used to protect the wearer. The rapidly moving cold air quickly dissipates the trapped body heat stored in the dead air spaces, intensifies the cooling effect caused by evaporation of perspiration, and can cause tremendous loss of body heat. Wind chill is one of the most dangerous threats to survival, not only in extreme cold conditions, but also in prolonged less rigorous cold conditions without proper protection. Approaches to help overcome "wind chill" include windproof or wind-resistant outer shell fabrics made with very tightly woven or knitted structures, specially laminated and wind resistant films or coatings that are applied to the outer shell fabrics. Impervious membranes, films or coatings that are applied to the inside of a fabric or coatings used as a bonding layer in a bi or tri-laminated fabric system are also common ways to address the wind chill problem.

## WINDPROOF:

A fabric's ability to totally block the penetration of wind and cold air into or through a garment. As in most products, there are degrees of "windproofness" ranging from totally impervious to all air penetration ('windproof') to providing a barrier against wind penetration ('wind resistant').

## YARN DYEING:

The technique of dyeing the yarns used to make cloth before they are knitted or woven into fabrics. Most multi-colored fabrics that are not printed, such as plaids and stripes, are made from dyed yarns.

## ZIRCONIUM CARBIDE MICROPARTICLES:

This sand-like material is sometimes bonded to a textile material to add an abrasion resistant surface to the fabric. These materials are next to diamonds in hardness. If the bonding material and the fabric to which these particles are bonded are strong enough, it is unlikely that the material would ever wear out through abrasion.

# INDEX

# INDEX

# INDEX

# INDEX

# INDEX

# INDEX

# INDEX